A GOURMET'S GUIDE

GENTLEMAN'S RELISH

A Compendium of English Culinary Oddities

A GOURMET'S GUIDE

GENTLEMAN'S RELISH

A Compendium of English Culinary Oddities

9 8 7 6 5 4 3 2 1

First published in 2007

Packaged by Susanna Geoghegan for
National Trust Books
151 Freston Road
London W10 6TH

An imprint of Anova Books Company Ltd

ISBN: 9781905400553

Printed in China by Hung Hing

INTRODUCTION

....

The recipe for Patum Peperium, The Gentleman's Relish®, has remained a closely guarded secret from the moment it was first devised by John Osborn in 1828. Since then this unique blend of anchovies, butter, herbs and spices has become established as one of the quintessential treats enjoyed by British gentlemen all over the world.

In this respect, The Gentleman's Relish® is not alone. Many dishes made popular in the nineteenth century, particularly those developed in India during the Raj, became firm favourites among male diners at home and abroad. At the same time British gentlemen pursued a fondness for the kind of comforting, wholesome food they enjoyed in the nursery as children, which then followed them into the wider world: to school at first, then to university or the armed forces, and finally into the gentleman's clubs of Mayfair and St James.

This varied menu augmented the time-honoured dishes that the male of the British species had been tucking into for generations. Game, fish, lamb, pork, beef and puddings had been staple fare for those who could afford them since the Middle Ages and they remain popular among gentlemen (and their families) today.

The same goes for the tipple that has accompanied this robust male fare – real ale, vintage claret, Black Velvet, decanter after decanter of mellow port – and the traditional cheeses, such as Stilton and Cheddar, that have provided sustenance and a savoury conclusion to meals for centuries.

In the pages that follow these and dozens of other foods and drinks that gentlemen relish are described and detailed in recipes, anecdotes and historical snippets. Together they present an introduction to a gentleman's well-stocked pantry and cellar, where there is much to inspire and even more to enjoy.

British gentlemen, who are fortunate enough to be landowners as well, have long taken pride in dining off the produce of their estates. Visitors seeking inspiration and enjoyment from a well-stocked pantry would surely admire the example set by Sir Denzil Onslow, who feasted his guests in great style at his fine estate at Purford near Ripley. The diarist, John Evelyn, attended one of Sir Denzil's dinner parties in 1681 and made the entry opposite in his diary …

'Much company and such an extraordinary feast as I had hardly ever seen at any country gentleman's table. What made it more remarkable was that there was not anything save what his estate about it did afford: as venison, rabbits, hares, pheasants partridges, pigeons, quails, poultrie, all sortes of fowl in season from his owne decoy neere his house, and all sorts of fresh fish.'

THE GENTLEMAN'S RELISH®

Discerning gentlemen (and some inquisitive ladies it has to be said) have been savouring the spiced anchovy paste known as Patum Peperium, The Gentleman's Relish®, ever since its recipe was first devised by one John Osborn in 1828. Spread sparingly on thin, hot toast buttered with unsalted butter, this quintessential English delicacy still evokes an era of elegant wining and dining when the savoury course was an essential component of every banquet and dinner.

'Unorthodox gastronomically, I suppose, and abhorred by the serious wine-lover, the small savoury nevertheless often makes an admirable ending to a meal, like some unexpected witticism or amusing epigram at the close of a pleasant conversation.' That, at least, is how Ambrose Heath endorsed the gentleman's penchant for savouries in his 1934 work on the subject, *Good Savouries*.

Bonne bouche par excellence

By this time, of course, savouries featured at the end of a meal, whereas in the eighteenth century snacks of anchovies and cheese had been served as appetisers before the serious eating began. Elisabeth Ayrton, author of *The Cookery of England* comments, 'Ladies very often missed the savoury, their delicate appetites already sated on the seven or so courses which might have preceded it.'

Anchovies feature prominently in savoury recipes, offering a piquant dimension to a variety of other ingredients. For the purist, though, there is nothing to beat straightforward anchovy toast – which many now enjoy at any time of the day when they feel the need for a *bonne bouche* to add a little zest to life.

Ancient origins

Mrs Beeton (1836–1865), writing in her classic *Book of Household Management*, observed that anchovy-based savouries, such as Patum Peperium, enabled 'gentlemen at wine-parties to enjoy their port with redoubled gusto'. She also quoted the author of *British Fishes*, who explans that the enthusiasm for anchovy paste had been enjoyed since ancient times: 'the anchovy is a common fish in the Mediterranean, from Greece to Gibralta, and was well known to the Greeks and Romans, by whom the liquor prepared from it, called *garum*, was in great estimation'.

By all accounts *garum* was a rather smelly concoction, unlike The Gentleman's Relish®, which has long been held as an icon of refined dining. Such is its prestige, that the recipe is known to only one employee of the licensed company, Elsenham Quality Foods, at any one time.

WORCESTERSHIRE SAUCE

Practically indigestible on its own, Worcestershire Sauce is one of those almost mystical ingredients, which works its magic in combination with many different types of food and drink – making it as indispensable in the cocktail cabinet as it is in the kitchen cupboard.

The original sauce was discovered by accident in the late 1830s, when John Lea and William Perrins, two Worcestershire chemists, were commissioned to recreate a spicy condiment that had lingered on the taste buds of Lord Sandys since his days in India as Governor of Bengal.

Eye-wateringly ghastly

Perhaps the initial result might have been more successful if he had engaged two chefs. As it was, the concoction Lea and Perrins produced was eye-wateringly ghastly, and was hastily dispatched to a cellar to be forgotten. It was only when it was stumbled upon again three years later during a clear out that it was re-tasted, and found to be transformed. A three-year maturation period has been built into the manufacture of Lea and Perrins' ever since.

First marketed at the beginning of Queen Victoria's reign, the definitive recipe remains a well-kept trade secret. The ingredients include molasses, sugar, salt, anchovies, tamarind extract, fresh onions, fresh garlic, spice and flavouring. These are fermented in malt vinegar (made from barley) over a long period of time and once matured the mixture is strained into wooden casks and left again to further mature. Even after further straining, some solids remain, which is why the bottle label tells you to 'shake well before use'.

A plethora of uses

And when it comes to use, it's hard to know where to start and where to stop. Soups, stews, meats, fish, poultry, cheese dishes, vegetable dishes, marinades, sauces, gravies and dressings can all be enhanced with varying amounts of Worcestershire Sauce.

Mixed with drinks, it gives the piquant kick to a Bloody Mary and picks you up the morning after in the uniquely disgusting Prairie Oyster – which, if you are fortunate enough to be unfamiliar with it, is made from mixing these ingredients:

1tsp Worcestershire Sauce
2 dashes vinegar
1tsp tomato sauce
1 dash pepper
1 egg yolk

Put into a small wine glass and float the egg yolk on top. Close your eyes and down in one!

TIPSY CAKE

More a dessert than a cake, Tipsy Cake was enjoyed by eighteenth-century bucks (who seldom turned away anything with a whiff of alcohol) and was traditionally served at ball suppers. Tipsy Cake had the further appeal of using up cake that had gone stale.

Ingredients

1 large sponge cake (3 or 4 days old)
Enough sweet wine or sherry to saturate it
  (about 350ml)
6tbsp brandy

50g sweet almonds
600ml rich custard
Ratafias or macaroons

Directions

Cut the bottom of the cake, so that it sits flat and firm in the serving dish. Make a small hole in the centre and pour in and over the cake sufficient wine, or sherry, mixed with the brandy, to soak the cake nicely. Allow 2 hours for the cake to become suitably soaked, occasionally spooning over it the wine/sherry and brandy mixture.

Blanch and cut the almonds into strips and stick them all over the cake when it is well soaked. Pour the custard round the base of the cake and garnish with ratafias or macaroons.

SLOE GIN

Never mind the first warming sip, the colour alone of Sloe Gin (dark red and irresistible) is enough to keep the cold at bay and put a rosy gloss on horizontal rain and scything wind. Sloe Gin is a winter tipple, handy in a hip flask on a bracing day outside, cosy and comforting after dark beside a crackling fire.

Ingredients

450g sloes • 1 bottle of gin • 350g granulated white sugar

Directions

After picking your sloes wash them well, place them in a suitable container and freeze them for at least a couple of days. This will make them burst.

Make sure the sloes are thoroughly defrosted before adding to the gin. Decant them into a sterilized one-litre bottle, pour in the sugar and then add the gin, filling the bottle to the neck. Seal it firmly with a cork or screw cap and place the bottle in a warm dark place, like an airing cupboard, for at least three months. For the first two weeks give it a good shake from time to time.

After three months, strain the fluid through a muslin cloth into another sterilized bottle, seal this and allow to mellow for a further six months before sampling. Be patient: it's well worth the wait.

OXFORD MARMALADE

Hungry Victorian undergraduates, eager for something more appetizing than the food served up in college halls, popularized Cooper's Oxford Marmalade after it first went on sale in 1874.

Although Frank Cooper became the driving force behind the branded product that still bears his name, it was his wife, Sarah, who created it. She had been brought up in Scotland, where marmalade had been eaten for breakfast since the eighteenth century. At the back of her husband's shop on Oxford's High Street, where Frank traded as a Specialist Grocer and Tea Dealer, Sarah used the Seville oranges he sold to make a dark, thick cut marmalade for the Cooper family. In 1874, though, she rather over-estimated how much they would consume, so Frank packed the surplus into earthenware jars and sold it in the shop, where passing students were quick to latch on to it and sales boomed.

Production continued at the High Street shop until 1903, when marmalade making moved to a purpose-built factory close to both of Oxford's railway stations. By then Cooper's could proudly advertise that it supplied marmalade to royalty and that the Prince of Wales was a patron.

Still perfect after seventy years

Promoting themselves as the sole manufacturer of 'Oxford' marmalade by the end of the nineteenth century (their telegram address read 'Marmalade, Oxford'), Cooper's sold direct to their customers by rail, as well as through their own shop.

The company built up a sizeable export business too, supplying marmalade and jams to expatriate and service breakfast tables around the globe. In 1910 a consignment of Cooper's Oxford Marmalade sailed south with Captain Scott and his party on their ill-fated expedition to become the first men to reach the South Pole. In 1980 one of these tins of marmalade was discovered in perfect condition by another expedition, which returned it to the manufacturers seventy years after they had despatched it from their premises to Scott's ship, the *Terra Nova*.

The Dundee connection

Dark, thick cut and distinctive, Oxford Marmalade is a variant of Dundee Marmalade, created once again by the enterprising wife of a local tradesman (one Janet Keiller). When her husband acquired a bargain-load of bitter oranges shipped to Dundee from Spain in the early years of the eighteenth century, Mrs Keiller speeded the manufacturing process by shredding the peel rather than pounding the fruit to a pulp, as earlier recipes dictated. By also keeping her marmalade less dense than others, she produced many more pots to the pound – and secured its enduring breakfast popularity by making it easy to spread on toast.

Keiller was known as the 'Marmalade Millionaire' and used his fortune from the sticky sales to fund one of his passions, archaeology. He bought, excavated and re-erected much of the prehistoric stone circle at Avebury in Wiltshire, a nearby rival to Stonehenge, and the museum there bears his name.

FUDGE

....

There is a story about how this delectable sweet got its name. It describes a happy accident in which a batch of caramels went wrong resulting in a softer, creamier set. The original idea was 'fudged', or 'merged together'.

The fudge recipe can have different flavourings and ingredients added to it, for example: dried fruit, nuts, chocolate, rum and other spirits. The basic recipe is usually flavoured with vanilla. In the West Country, cream, sometimes clotted cream, is used to make an even more wickedly tempting confection.

Ingredients

450g granulated sugar • 275ml double or whipping cream • 150ml milk
50g unsalted butter • 1tbsp water • 1tsp vanilla essence

Directions

Place all the ingredients (except the vanilla) into a thick-based pan over a low heat and stir until the sugar has completely dissolved. Increase the heat and bring the solution to a boil and continue to boil until a little dropped into a cup of cold water makes a soft ball when rolled between the finger tips (about ten minutes). Remove the pan from the heat and allow it to settle for a moment or two. Stir in the vanilla essence and then beat the mixture until it becomes thick and creamy. Pour into a thick lined tray and leave to set. Cut into squares.

BUTTERSCOTCH

This traditional sweet is similar to toffee but the syrup is boiled at a lower temperature before setting. The ingredients are sugar, butter and water, milk or cream. Until the middle of the twentieth century many recipes included whisky. This may account for the name, along with a tradition that it was a Scottish speciality.

Nowadays butterscotch sauces are very popular with desserts and can simply be poured over ice creams or pancakes or incorporated into fruit tarts and puddings. The recipe below, however, is for the old fashioned confectionery.

Ingredients

450g demerara sugar • 110g butter
300ml milk • 1–2tsp vanilla essence

Directions

Gently heat the sugar, butter and milk in a saucepan, stirring until the sugar has completely dissolved. Bring the heat up and boil the mixture until it forms a brittle thread when a little is dropped into a cup of cold water. Remove from the heat and carefully stir in the vanilla essence. Again taking great care, pour the syrup into an oiled tray. When it has cooled somewhat, mark the butterscotch into squares and break when it is set hard.

MELTON MOWBRAY PORK PIE

Strange though it may seem today, many a young Regency buck would have been very gratified to find himself described as a 'Tip Top Meltonian'. It meant you had really made your mark amongst your peers as a fearless rider to hounds. Melton Mowbray was the centre for the renowned Quorn Hunt, attracting young aristocrats from all over the country who indulged in some riotous goings-on when in their cups after a day's sport, and their presence may have accounted for the development in the area of one of Britain's delicacies.

A-hunting we will go

By the early nineteenth century, pork pies were popular with huntsmen who would put one (or two) in their saddlebags before riding out for the day. The pastry was not then intended for eating; in the absence of plastic food containers it was used simply to encase the meat. The filling was eaten and the pastry thrown away, although it was not long before the wonderfully rich and satisfying crust was considered as much a delicacy as the succulent pork packed inside. In more sedate settings, the pies frequently graced the high-tea table, sitting temptingly in the middle of the lace tablecloth.

Accept no substitutes

Some things are definitely worth fighting for and in recent years the pie-makers of Melton Mowbray (and its environs) in Leicestershire have been up in arms after becoming increasingly concerned that any old pork pie was being passed off as a Melton Mowbray. Uniformly straight-sided pies with a pink,
minced pork filling are very different to the original article. A Melton Mowbray Pork Pie Association was formed and the EU petitioned in order to safe-guard the product's good name. There is even a website in existence to help you distinguish between a real Melton Mowbray and imitations. So, no pink, minced pork – the meat should look a little grey because it should be un-cured, and coarsely chopped, not minced. The hot water crust must be 'hand-raised' around the outside of a mould and not enclosed in a container. This means that, as the pie cooks, it will belly out a little to give a distinctively rounded contour. The pastry should also be made using lard (pork fat) and between it and the meat filling is a layer of jellied stock again, preferably, rendered from pork. This is poured through a hole in the pie's lid after baking and settles around the meat filling, which will have shrunk away from the pastry crust as it cooked. Flavourings can vary a little, ranging from a simple seasoning of salt and pepper, to the addition of herbs, mild spices and a dash of anchovy essence.

GROUSE

In season from 12 August until the beginning of December, British grouse come from the upland moors of northern England and Scotland. This is how Mrs Beeton suggested preparing them for the table:

> Let the birds hang as long as possible; pluck and draw them; wipe, but do not wash them, inside and out, and truss them without the head, the same as for a roast fowl. Many persons still continue to truss them with the head under the wing, but the former is now considered the most approved method. Put them down to a sharp clear fire; keep them well basted the whole of the time they are cooking, and serve them on a buttered toast, soaked in the dripping-pan, with a little melted butter poured over them, or with bread-sauce and gravy.

> *Time*—$\frac{1}{2}$ hour; if liked very thoroughly done, 35 minutes.

BUCK'S FIZZ

Today Buck's Fizz is a universally popular cocktail, enjoyed throughout the day but particularly at breakfast, when it provides a refreshing and stimulating introduction to whatever delights lie in store.

The original Buck's Fizz was created by Captain H J Buckmaster, the founder of the private gentleman's club, Buck's in Mayfair. Buck's Club still guards the original recipe, which is said to contain three further ingredients that are additional to the standard mix of orange juice and champagne. For those unable to sample the genuine article, however, the popular form of Buck's Fizz is still a delightful drink.

Directions

Mix half-and-half well-chilled champagne and fresh orange juice. Optional additions include 2½tsp cognac, or 1tsp grenadine.

LAVERBREAD

Porphyra umbilicalis is an unlikely looking raw ingredient used in both Japan, where it forms part of the national cuisine called sushi, and in Wales, where it is made into laverbread.

For anyone unfamiliar with this interesting international delicacy, it is a seaweed that lies in thin, one-cell thick strands, plastered over rocks as the tide recedes. It has been eaten in Britain for hundreds of years, the first known written record being found in Camden's *Britannica* of 1607, which provides a description of the springtime harvest of 'Lhawvan' from a Pembrokeshire beach.

Collecting the seaweed was hard work and not necessarily straightforward, as it sometimes disappeared from one site to reappear the following season at

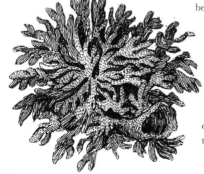

another. Traditionally it was collected manually between October and May from rocks lying in the sand along the tidal margin and loaded onto patient donkeys. It was then hand washed to clean off the sand before being boiled for a long time in pans over coal fires. The black, jelly-like substance that resulted from this process was usually eaten combined with oatmeal or spread thinly on toast.

During the eighteenth century the popularity of laverbread increased along with the development of the coal mining industry, and it became a staple food for the miners. A traditional Welsh breakfast consists of a mixture of laverbread, cockles and bacon, and it is generally recommended to cook laverbread in bacon fat as the flavours complement one another well.

Modern analysis shows that it is an extraordinarily good food, containing more than fifty known minerals and trace elements essential for maintaining a healthy body, providing high quantities of iodine, iron and calcium. It is also packed with protein whilst possessing an extremely low calorie count.

Although a very Welsh food, nowadays a lot of laverbread comes from Scotland. However, Swansea market still has several stalls selling only laverbread and cockles harvested from the Gower Peninsula.

A traditional Welsh breakfast accompaniment can be made like this:

Ingredients

100g fresh or tinned laverbread
25g medium or fine oatmeal

Directions

Mix the laverbread and oatmeal together and shape into cakes about the size and shape of rissoles. Place them into hot bacon fat and fry for 2–3 minutes on each side then remove and serve them with other breakfast ingredients.

MIXED GRILL

Over the centuries England's old chop houses, grill rooms and taverns became celebrated for satisfying the hearty appetites of their clients with what would become one of an Englishman's favourite meals.

Ingredients

Serves: 4

4 lamb cutlets, trimmed of excess fat

4 lamb kidneys, skinned, halved & cored

4 small beef steaks

4 small gammon steaks (or 4 rashers of streaky bacon, rinds removed)

4 pork sausages

225g black pudding, cut into 4 slices

4 large tomatoes, halved

4 large mushrooms, peeled

2tbsp olive oil

Salt and freshly ground black pepper

Directions

Prepare a charcoal grill, or pre-heat a grill to its hottest. Brush the chops, kidney halves, cutlets and steaks with olive oil and season with salt and pepper.

Grill the sausages and kidneys first for eight to ten minutes, turning frequently. Grill the lamb cutlets and gammon or bacon for five to six minutes. Then grill the steaks and black pudding for two to three minutes on each side. Add tomatoes and mushrooms and brush with hot fat from the pan.

Arrange on a serving dish and spoon the fat-skimmed pan juices over the meats.

MULLIGATAWNY SOUP

In the reign of Queen Elizabeth I a group of gentlemen investors formed a trading company that was to become the occupying power in India until it handed the rule of the subcontinent back to the Crown in 1858. Up to that time The East India Company, or 'John Company' as it became known, colonized the country, exporting much of its natural wealth overseas and, in particular, back to Britain.

A favourite at home and abroad

By the time the rule of the East India Company rule gave way to that of the British Raj, mulligatawny soup was a firm favourite with both the ex-patriot British and 'old India hands' back home. The recipe, which originated from the Madras area in the south-east of India, was devised by local cooks during the time that the East India Company held sway in the sub-continent. The whole concept of soup being British, rather than Indian, the somewhat curious name derives from the Tamil *milagu tanni*, 'pepper water' – a spirited attempt to put an Indian title to this alien form of food.

There seems to be as many variations of the recipe as there were cooks, each having his own version of the basic, spicy concoction – some produced a clear liquid, some a thicker soup. The one given below is based on Elizabeth Acton's version, dating from 1840.

Ingredients

3 large onions, chopped

110g butter

700g peeled marrow or courgettes

1 tin of tomatoes

1 large potato, chopped

425ml beef or chicken stock

1tbsp Worcestershire Sauce

1tsp Madras curry powder

240ml long grain rice

Salt and black pepper to taste

Directions

Melt the butter in large saucepan, add the onions and cook until golden brown. Dice the marrow or courgettes and add to the onions with the potato and tinned tomatoes. Season, add the curry powder and simmer in a covered pan for about half an hour. Cook the rice separately until tender. Liquidize the vegetables, pour into a pan and add the rice, the stock and Worcestershire Sauce. Adjust the seasoning to taste. Lemon or lime juice may also be added, as can apple, coconut, mango chutney or yoghurt.

CLOTTED CREAM

Unforgettable and unforgiving, clotted cream is one of those treats that everyone should indulge in just occasionally – if only to recall the taste and sensation which seems to epitomise a bygone era.

Clotted cream is traditionally a product of the rich pasturelands of England's West Country, where Cornish and Devonshire cream teas form part of a quintessential English afternoon. It is produced by cooking double cream to just below its boiling point. This concentrates its fat content and develops a distinctive yellow crust as it cools.

Serving suggestions

When added to scones spread with strawberry jam, the combination is delicious and lives in the memory long after the small indulgence has passed. Clotted cream, with a consistency similar to soft butter, can also be used as a replacement for butter in making such things as toffees. It can be spread on freshly baked bread with honey or jam; and when served with black treacle the contrasting colours give the mixture the evocative name: thunder and lightning.

STICKY TOFFEE PUDDING

As steamed puddings go, Sticky Toffee Pudding goes as well as any. After a spell in the dietary doldrums, this utterly addictive, calorie-intense pudding is enjoying a revival at home and is spearheading an interest in traditional English desserts abroad.

From north-west to West End

Today you can find it on menus in top West End restaurants, where it arrives as mouthwatering and sinfully delicious as it would have done in its original home in the north-west of England. The only difference is that in the West End you're as likely to be offered a dollop of vanilla ice-cream, crème fraiche or clotted cream to go with it in addition to (or possibly instead of) a traditional coating of custard.

The distinctive flavour and texture of Sticky Toffee Pudding comes from the puréed dates that are added to the sponge mix. As for the tempting toffee – that only makes an appearance in the sauce.

PICKLED WALNUTS

Archaeological excavations from Périgord in south-west France have revealed that our Neolithic ancestors were roasting walnuts over 8,000 years ago. By the time the classical civilizations of Greece and Rome were flourishing there were written accounts of planting walnut orchards; in fact the Latin name for the nut is translated as 'Jupiter's acorn'. It wasn't until the sixteenth century, however, that walnut trees were a feature of European cultivation. The English name comes from the German *Wallnuss* or 'foreign nut' – foreign in origin, perhaps, but quickly absorbed into our way of life to become a British favourite.

Polarized reactions

Autumn is the time to harvest walnuts for eating, but if they are intended for pickling the harvest takes place much earlier in the summer, before the shells have hardened. The way to test the softness of the shell is to spear each with a darning needle, which shouldn't meet any resistance as it is pushed inside. The walnuts are not peeled or shelled before the pickling process begins. The whole of the green globe goes into the brine from which it emerges black, moist and something of a challenge to those who are not fans. There is nothing else quite like pickled walnuts and they tend to polarize reactions – people either love them or hate them.

Pickled walnuts can be served at any time but are particularly popular at Christmas, accompanying Stilton cheese and cold meats. The following recipe can be followed for pickling walnuts at home.

Ingredients

Brine made with 100g salt to 1litre of water

For every 2kg walnuts:

1 litre brewed malt vinegar

500g brown sugar

1tsp allspice

1tsp cloves

1tsp grated ginger

½tsp cinnamon

1–2 black peppercorns

Directions

Pick the whole walnuts in the summer, as described above, and prick them with a fork. Wear gloves for both operations as the juice stains. Immerse the nuts, still intact, in the brine and soak for one week, drain and repeat for another week. Drain once more, place on trays and leave to dry. They will start to turn black – this is normal. Make up the pickling liquor with the vinegar, sugar and spices, bring to the boil and simmer the nuts for about fifteen minutes. Allow to cool and bottle. Store in a cool dark place for about a month before eating.

BOMBAY DUCK

Bombay Duck, a popular side order to accompany curry, is actually a fish (*Harpodon nehereus*) caught in the seas and estuaries of India. It is long, thin and rather strange looking, with a protruding lower jaw. If it is to be sold locally the fish is simply split and dried. If it is to be exported, it is split along its length, filleted and flattened. Then it is immersed in a salt solution and left to dry in the sun, hanging on scaffolds of bamboo poles. After a couple of days the fish is taken down and put between rollers to flatten it further and then hung out to dry once again.

Neither fish nor fowl

So, how did a fish become a duck? As is so often the case with names that originated in India a degree of linguistic confusion intervened; in this instance one centred on the Indian postal service. Initially much of the dried fish was distributed around the country on Bombay mail trains, which got a reputation for being very smelly as a result. The Hindi word for 'mail' is *dak*, which became corrupted by the British into 'duck', so giving Bombay Duck its rather ambiguous name.

ANGELS ON HORSEBACK

This hot appetizer dates to the Victorian era when oysters were consumed by a much wider spectrum of society than today. The engaging name apparently derives from the fact that the oysters curl when cooked and look like a small pair of wings. Fans of the 1970s series *Charlie's Angels* – and there are many of them – will recall an episode called 'Angels on Horseback' in which the girls, often inappropriately dressed for riding, sleuthed on a dude ranch.

To make a more substantial snack, Angels on Horseback can be served on toast.

Ingredients

A dozen fresh oysters, removed from their shells
6 rashers of rindless streaky bacon
Salt and pepper

Directions

Preheat the grill to a moderate heat. Cut each bacon rasher in half, wrap around each oyster and season. Pack them together tightly in a shallow baking tray. Cook under the grill for about five minutes, turning once.

BRANSTON PICKLE

The name is so familiar it is probable that few people stop to think, 'Why *Branston*?'

Those who do bother to enquire discover that this hugely popular pickle is actually named after an attractive east Staffordshire village on the banks of the Trent and Mersey canal, just south of Burton-on-Trent. It was there that Crosse & Blackwell first produced their famous product in 1922.

The rise of Crosse & Blackwell

A couple of centuries before that, a grocery business called West and Wyatt had been established on the site of the old Shaftesbury Theatre in London. This was bought by two young men named Edmund Crosse and Thomas Blackwell, and it was they who were responsible for the rapid expansion of the business to the point where it, and many of its products, became household names.

The company they founded enjoyed its heyday in the 1950s when no British dinner table was complete without being graced by some condiment bearing a Crosse and Blackwell label. A clever marketing idea resulted an advertising slogan that referred to the company practice of carrying out a taste test every morning: 'Ten O'Clock Tested' became a national catchphrase.

Christmas panic

In recent years, Branston Pickle was being made at a factory near Bury St Edmunds, and when this suffered a devastating fire in late October 2004, production came to a halt whilst rebuilding took place. When the news got out that the company estimated they only had stocks to last two weeks, there was consternation amongst Branston's countless fans and panic buying was detected in stores across the country. The thought of Christmas and no rich, dark, tangy pickle to accompany the Stilton and cold turkey was too much for some; on eBay alone jars of Branston Pickle were changing hands for as much as £16 apiece.

Trade secret

The recipe for Branston Pickle has always been a closely guarded secret; there are spices, dates, brown sugar and the mysterious rutabaga (or, less mysteriously, the swede). Whatever the secret is, it is a recipe for success: 28,000,000 jars are sold annually in Britain, and amongst its devotees are model Naomi Campbell and Hollywood film star Catherine Zeta-Jones.

KENDAL MINT CAKE

There is a cherished story concerning the origins of Kendal Mint Cake that tells of a Victorian confectioner who set out to make glacier mints one day. He became distracted by some other piece of business and by the time he returned to his task the sugar mixture had become grainy and brown. Being the sort of man who didn't like to waste anything, he poured the mix into some cooling trays anyway, and left it to set – and in so doing the famous mint cake was born.

The man credited with the discovery was Joseph Wiper, who went into the production of mint cake in Kendal in 1869. Local customers spread the word and before long weekly shipments of his sweet were being despatched from Kendal Station to other outlets in the North. When old Mr Wiper retired to British Columbia in 1910 he left his descendants to carry on the Wiper business, which included Shackleton's 1914 trans-Antarctic expedition among their customers.

Munching mint cake at the top of the world

Sam Clarke, another Kendal man in the sweet trade, had been invalided out of the forces after serving his country in the First World War. He purchased a recipe for mint cake and began manufacturing his own, naming his company Romney's, after the great eighteenth-century portrait painter, George Romney, who had also lived and learnt his trade in Kendal. Part of their marketing campaign was to advertise in climbing magazines, a strategy fully vindicated when the firm was contacted by the 1953 Everest team, who wondered if Romney's could supply

them with enough mint cake for their historic expedition. There were a few difficulties to overcome; one was that the expedition needed the cake within a week, another that it had to be packed to withstand high-altitude conditions and lastly, sweet rationing was still in force. The first two conditions were met and as to the last, Romney's staff patriotically gave up their own sweet ration coupons to aid the cause! Having reached the summit of Everest, Hilary and Tensing rewarded themselves with Romney's Mint Cake, a fact that did no harm to sales back home.

Time-honoured traditions

Romney's bought Wiper's in 1987 but still use the Wiper's name and method of production alongside their own. And the secret of their success? That would be telling – but eighty-year-old copper pans, the best peppermint oils from the USA, Brazil and China and the subtle blending of these with sugar and glucose have something to do with it.

BATH OLIVER BISCUITS

For a clever and ambitious young doctor, early eighteenth-century Bath had much to commend it. The spa town was rapidly developing as a social centre that attracted the rich and influential, who flocked to Bath to take its curative waters. In their wake followed physicians offering treatments and cures of their own. Such a man was William Oliver, who had studied medicine at the universities of Cambridge and Leyden, before establishing his first medical practice in Plymouth. Oliver moved to Bath in 1728 and was soon doing very well for himself both professionally and socially. He moved into a fine house on Queen's Square and mixed with the likes of Alexander Pope, man of letters, and Beau Nash, man of fashion. The doctor himself was elected a Fellow of the Royal Society in 1729.

From bun to biscuit

It seems that there was an endearingly domestic side to Dr Oliver, for he is credited with inventing the Bath Bun, which he freely 'prescribed' to his patients. They, naturally enough, loved these generously proportioned, sticky, sugar-topped cakes and tucked into them with no thought to the inevitable weight gain that followed. Their physician was, however, disconcerted by the results and set about creating a plainer snack that would have a more beneficial effect. So it was that the Bath Oliver biscuit, so delicious with savouries and cheese, came to be.

A generous bequest

Dr William Oliver was one of the founders of the Bath General Hospital (now Royal National Hospital for Rheumatic Diseases) and was elected physician to the Hospital in 1740, retiring in 1761. He died three years later. Fortunately, the Bath Oliver did not die with him. The good doctor had a coachman called Atkins to whom he bequeathed his secret recipe, and was thoughtful enough also to leave him a sack of flour and enough money start up in biscuit production himself. Atkins took up the challenge and became a wealthy man in his own right.

More than a century later the Bath Oliver business passed to James Fortt, the name that we now see on that distinctive white packaging.

STILTON CHEESE

It was an American, Clifton Fadiman, who described cheese as 'milk's leap toward immortality' – and when one contemplates a gloriously mature Stilton, one can appreciate his sentiment. Blue-veined like a true aristocrat, sitting all alone on a plate with perhaps a small glass of port near to hand, it will bring a feeling of contentment to many who just have room left after a good meal for something sublimely savoury.

A mark of exclusivity

Even in this age of mass production and imitation only six dairies are licensed to make it according to the original recipe and it is unique among British cheeses in having its own trademark and PDO, having been granted "protected designation origin" by the European Commission. Today Stilton cheese is produced exclusively in the three counties of Nottinghamshire, Derbyshire and Leicestershire.

It may come as a surprise to learn, though, that one place it was never produced was Stilton. This large village on the Great North Road, which provided a welcome break in the eighteenth century for coach travellers heading north from London, is situated close to Melton Mowbray and villages such as Wymondham, where the famous cheese was actually made. It was sold to hungry guests at old coaching inns at Stilton, such as The Bell and The Angel. Its prime position in the national transport system meant that Stilton became the main distribution centre for the cheese, which before long assumed the name of the place where it could be bought rather than where it was made.

The taste of excellence

A few names come down to us over the years as being closely associated with the development of the cheese. The principal recipe was passed from one generation to the next in the Beaumont family of Quenby in Leicestershire. Frances Pawlett of Wymondham set a standard of excellence with her Stilton making and she, her husband, and the landlord of The Bell Inn formed a highly successful marketing team.

Stilton cheeses mature in the dairy for ten weeks before reaching the retailers and can continue to mature for six weeks after that. If eaten young, the texture will be crumbly and the taste, fresh. The longer it is left before consumption the more the cheese turns yellow, acquiring a riper buttery taste.

The distinctive blue veining, like a marble-topped table, is initiated after the cheeses have been maturing for about six weeks. Stainless steel needles are pushed into them to allow in air along with blue mould *Penicillium glaucum*, which spreads throughout the cheese creating the special appearance of Stilton.

SWAN

'But these are they of which ye shall not eat … The little owl, and the great owl, and the swan.' Tell that to the Tudors (or just about any well-to-do person in the past), who blithely ignored this biblical injunction. Swan was definitely on the menu. Even as late as 1874, Queen Victoria's son Prince Leopold sent a swan to his tutor at Oxford for his family to feast on at Christmas.

The mute swan is this country's most common swan and it came under royal protection as early as the twelfth century. After that any swan owned by a private individual that was found straying became forfeit to the crown. You had to be a wealthy individual or an institution of considerable status to qualify for swan ownership. Guilds, and colleges such as Eton, had the right to own swans and all owners would mark their young birds, or cygnets, with distinctive nicks in their beaks. This process of marking the birds is called swan upping and still takes place today, although private ownership of swans on the River Thames is now only maintained by the Dyers and Vintners companies, with all other swans on the river belonging to the Queen. In the first Queen Elizabeth's reign, anyone caught unlawfully driving away swans or stealing eggs faced a year's imprisonment and a fine.

The centerpiece of the feast

Being such a special bird, it was served with great ceremony and was placed as the centerpiece of a feast. Some cooks would give the roasted bird a gilded look by glazing it with flour, egg yolk and saffron. The more ambitious would stuff it with smaller, boned birds, usually beginning with an egg inside a quail, inside a pheasant, inside a duck and would serve it dressed up in its feathers, wings, and un-plucked neck and head (and lots of wire, one imagines, to support the outer 'decorations').

Here is a fourteenth-century recipe for roast swan with a sauce called chaudon:

For to dihyte a swan. Tak & vndo hym & wasch hym, & do on a spite & enarme hym fayre & roste hym wel; & dysmembre hym in the beste manere & mak a fayre chyne, & the sauce therto schal be mad in this manere, & it is clept:

Chaudon. Tak the issu of the swan & wasch it wel, & scoure the guttes wel with salt, & seth the issu al togedere til it be ynow, & then tak it vp and wasch it wel & hew it smal, & tak bred & poudere of gyngere & of galyngale & grynde togedere & tempere it with the broth, & coloure it with the blood. And when it is ysothe & ygrounde & streyned, salte it, & boyle it wel togydere in a postnet & sesen it with a litel vynegre.

(Galyngale is an old word for Cypress root, which was ground up and gave a gingery flavour.)

MARMITE

For hundreds, if not thousands, of years people had been fermenting sugars with yeast to make alcohol and throwing away the by-product. Then, in the nineteenth century, a German scientist called Justus von Liebig developed a foodstuff by concentrating and bottling brewer's yeast.

The French connection

Using Liebig's ideas, a company opened a factory at Burton-on-Trent (a centre for the brewing industry) in 1902, where they produced a dark, nutritious spread made from brewer's yeast extract mixed with vitamins, vegetable extracts and spices. This was originally sold in little earthenware pots, but in the 1920s the pots were replaced by the glass jars that have changed little over the subsequent decades. The picture on the present-day label shows a small covered casserole pot, known in France as a *marmite*, which gives a hint as to how the makers hit upon the iconic brand name for their distinctly British poduct.

The British armed forces in two world wars benefited from Marmite's high vitamin B content. In the First World War it was included in soldiers' rations and 'My Mate, Marmite' has been a welcome supplement for our boys (and, probably, girls) ever since. Back in Blighty, of course, it was establishing itself as a firm favourite, getting a big boost in popularity with the increasing awareness of the importance of vitamins in the nation's diet.

A feast for the imagination

About two thirds of the huge amount of Marmite sold in Britain every year ends up spread on hot buttered toast. A lot of the remaining third goes into sandwiches, but a small percentage is used more imaginatively in all the little, secret ways people have devised for enjoying this wonderfully savoury spread: Marmite roast potatoes, Marmite and bananas, Marmite and baked beans, Marmite and scrambled eggs, crisps dipped into the Marmite jar. One fully committed enthusiast, Paul Hartley, has written *The Marmite Cookbook*, which has sold more than 100,000 copies.

It is well known – and wholly acknowledged by the manufacturers themselves – that the British public is polarized over loving or loathing their iconic spread. The American author Bill Bryson clearly couldn't understand the appeal, in spite of living in England for many years, when he observed 'There are certain things that you have to be British, or at least older than me, or possibly both, to appreciate: skiffle music, salt-cellars with a single hole, and Marmite', which Bryson challengingly describes as 'an edible yeast extract with the visual properties of an industrial lubricant'.

KEDGEREE

This recipe started out in India as *khichri*, a combination of rice, lentils and spices, but as early as 1845 Eliza Acton was recommending the Anglicized Kedgeree in her *Modern Cookery for Private Families*, suggesting serving it with fresh fish such as cold turbot, brill, salmon or sole.

Kedgeree arrived in England at about the same time as regular supplies of smoked haddock brought by stagecoach from Scotland. The bland ingredients, rice and hard-boiled eggs, made Kedgeree a perfect counterpoint to the strong salty flavour of the preserved fish.

A smell to tease and tantalise

In its country of origin it was a popular breakfast dish, especially in the Bombay region, and it became a feature of Victorian and Edwardian breakfasts in Britain. Over the years Kedgeree was augmented by quartered hard-boiled eggs, and smoked haddock: cooked, broken into pieces and mixed with the lightly spiced rice. No sideboard was complete without a large dish of Kedgeree to start the day for guests enjoying a weekend country house party. As Elizabeth David commented in *Spices, Salt and Aromatics in the English Kitchen*, 'At the thought of a kedgeree made with smoked haddock and plenty of hard-boiled eggs, English eyes grow dreamy and the smell of an English country house dining room at breakfast time … comes back to tease and tantalise.'

Ingredients

250g smoked haddock
25g butter
225g long grain rice
1tsp garam masala or curry powder
2 hard-boiled eggs
Chopped parsley

Directions

Place the haddock in a pan with barely enough water to cover and gently poach for approximately ten minutes or until the flesh is just opaque and flakes easily. Drain and break the fish into pieces, discarding the skin and bones. Simmer the rice until cooked and drain well. Melt the butter in a pan and add the rice, haddock and garam masala or curry powder, stirring gently until well mixed with the butter and thoroughly heated. Transfer to a warm dish and garnish with the egg and sprinkle with the parsley.

SAMPHIRE

Rock samphire is also called sea fennel, although most agree that its taste when cooked is closest to asparagus. It has been collected and used in cooking and as a herbal remedy for centuries. Because it grows near to the seashore, on rocks and cliffs, it was associated with St Peter, patron saint of fishermen. Indeed, the name samphire may derive from Saint Pierre or San Pietra.

Very pleasant to taste and stomach

In days gone by it was either pickled to preserve it, or used fresh as a vegetable or in salads. Samphire could even be bought in its pickled state on the streets of London, where it was sold under the name 'Crest Marine'. The famous seventeenth-century herbalist Nicholas Culpeper lamented that even in his day samphire was no longer widely used, for 'it is a safe herb, very pleasant to taste and stomach'. Culpeper's predecessor, John Gerard, wrote the following in 1597: 'The leaves kept in pickle and eaten in salads with oil and vinegar is a pleasant sauce for meat, wholesome for the stoppings of the liver, milt and kidnies. It is the pleasantest sauce, most familiar and best agreeing with man's body.'

The plant is characterized by long fleshy leaves and clusters of small yellow flowers; the leaves are used for cooking, the flowers and woody base are discarded. Mrs M Grieve in her *Modern Herbal* stresses that 'the whole plant is aromatic and has a powerful scent'.

Recent revival

Gathering samphire from the seashore could be a hazardous occupation, especially if the bit you wanted was growing on the cliffs near Dover. This was where Shakespeare had in mind when he wrote in *King Lear*:

> 'Half-way down
> Hangs one that gathers samphire; dreadful trade!'

Samphire has enjoyed a revival in recent years and is not infrequently found on menus, especially in restaurants specializing in fish; the two complementing one another well. Rock samphire is relatively hard to find and marsh samphire, principally found around the coast of Norfolk, can be used as an alternative.

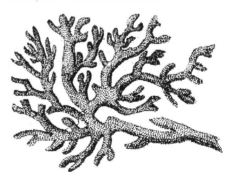

MUFFINS

The name given to these spongy white buns is very old, appearing in England around the time of the Norman Conquest. It is understandable, then, that 'muffin' derives from the French word *moufflet*, a soft-textured bread. English muffins are round, flat and made with yeast, quite unlike American muffins, which are more like cakes.

Traditionally muffins were served at teatime. They were split in half, toasted and spread with butter and jam. Some people split the muffin with a fork, giving a rougher surface, which becomes crunchier when toasted and traps the melting butter in little pockets. Before the development of toasters or even efficient grills, the muffin was speared with a toasting fork and held before the fire.

Food for all

Muffins started as something more or less relegated to the servants' hall, but gradually worked their way upstairs, where they became the mainstay of wintry nursery teas, or were served in drawing rooms, kept warm on a plate under a silver cover. They were also a welcome supplement to their otherwise meagre rations enjoyed by boys in their studies at boarding school, or by impoverished university students. At the same time ready-made muffins were sold in the street by 'muffin men', who carried their wares on wooden trays hanging from their necks.

Muffins can also be enjoyed as the base for savoury snacks, the best known being Eggs Benedict. Various stories surround the origin of this dish. One holds that an American, Samuel Benedict, suggested it to Oscar, the renowned chef of New York City's Waldorf-Astoria Hotel, hoping that the combination of ingredients might cure his hangover. It must be said that others lay claim to being the originators, but whoever was the genius behind it, Eggs Benedict has become a classic dish on both sides of the Atlantic.

Ingredients

To make one serving:
Hollandaise sauce
1 poached egg
1 smoked rasher of bacon or slice of ham
1 English muffin

Directions

Split and toast the muffin and place on a plate. Pile on the bacon or ham and top with the poached egg. Cover with the hollandaise sauce.

CUMBERLAND SAUCE

In spite of its apparent connection with north-west England, food historians believe that Cumberland Sauce was first concocted in Germany and was named after the son of King George V of Hanover, Crown Prince Ernst August II; as the great-grandson of King George III of England he also bore the title Duke of Cumberland.

Cumberland Sauce is served cold, most frequently with hot or cold ham, but it also goes well with cold tongue and game pie. It is thin in consistency and has a wonderfully fruity, winey flavour. As with many traditional sauces, some variations to the recipe have evolved over time – the one given below is a guide that can be altered according to taste.

Ingredients

100g good quality redcurrant jelly
Rind and juice of 2 oranges
Rind and juice of 1 lemon

4tbsp port wine
2tsp Dijon mustard
Pinch ground ginger (optional)

Directions

Heat the jelly and fruit rinds and juice in a pan, adding the mustard (with the ginger if using), and stirring frequently until the jelly has melted. Pour in the port and bring up to heat. Leave until cold before serving.

LAMB'S WOOL

Lamb's Wool is a warm winter drink that dates from the Middle Ages when it formed part of the traditional feasting held on Twelfth Night, the last night of the Christmas festivities. The drink probably gets its name from the whiteness of the roasted apples, which are floated on the surface of the mixture of cider (sometimes with beer added) sugar and spices.

Ingredients

Makes 8 servings:

6 cored baking apples • 2tbsp brown sugar

2 litres cider, or a mixture of cider and beer • pinch of nutmeg

$\frac{1}{4}$tsp cinnamon • $\frac{1}{4}$tsp ground ginger

Directions

Roast the apples until they are soft and about to burst. Alternatively, you can peel and boil them until they are soft and flaky. Once ready, you can either leave the apples whole, or break them up.

Pour the cider, or cider and beer mixture, into a large bowl and gradually add sugar, tasting for sweetness. Add the spices. Bring to the boil and simmer for 10–15 minutes. Pour the liquid over the apples in a large punch bowl and serve in cups or mugs.

SCHWEPPES INDIAN TONIC WATER

Jean Jacob Schweppe was born in Germany in 1740 but whilst still a young man moved to Geneva. He was a watchmaker by trade and also a keen amateur scientist. It was this interest that eventually led him to pioneer the commercial production of carbonated mineral water. Schweppe set up his own company in 1783, while still living in Switzerland, before moving to premises in London in 1790. During the next decade Schweppes carbonated waters gained in popularity and the medical profession began recommending them to patients suffering from kidney and bladder problems and to those with gout and digestive troubles. By the 1830s Schweppes was supplying the Royal Household with their soda and mineral waters.

An iconic British drink

The medicinal properties of another Schweppes product gave rise to an iconic British drink. Mineral water was an important commodity for the colonial British living in Africa and the Orient, where malaria was an ever-present threat. Schweppes added a large dollop of quinine to the water they sent out to these parts of the empire, as a way of protecting their customers from contracting malaria. Originally, what became known as tonic water, was just water and quinine and much more bitter to the taste than its modern equivalent; the tonic we add to our gin today has only a hint of quinine and is also sweetened.

Holy bark – real bite

The beneficial effects of quinine were first noticed by Father Agostino Salumbrino, a Jesuit priest living in Lima, Peru in the late sixteenth and early seventeenth centuries. The local Quechua Indians used the bark of the cinchona tree as a muscle relaxant to stop the shivering brought on by intense cold. They called the bark *Quina-quina* or 'holy bark' which is how the medicine got its name. Salumbrino sent a sample of it back to Italy where it was found to be very effective in the treatment of malaria.

What started as something good for the health is still something very good for the spirit – in both senses of the word. Tonic water not only makes a superlative mixer, but poured over ice with a hint of lemon and lime, it's a thirst quencher with real 'bite'.

WHITEBAIT

Whitebait are the small fry of herring and sprats which used to be netted in large quantities in the River Thames, beside which whitebait feasts were popular events. Whitebait are still caught at the mouth of the estuary at Southend, where a Whitebait Festival takes place annually in the early autumn to celebrate and give blessing for the first catch.

Ingredients

Serves: 4

450g Whitebait • Seasoned flour • Oil

Salt • Lemon, cut into wedges • Freshly chopped parsley

Directions

Wash and dry the fish and coat in seasoned flour. Heat the oil and put about a quarter of the fish in the frying basket. Shake out any loose flour.

Deep fry until crisp, about three to four minutes. Remove the fish from the pan to a warmed serving dish and continue to cook the remaining whitebait. When all are done, return the fish to the basket and fry for a few seconds in very hot oil to crisp them up. Drain well on kitchen towel, sprinkle with salt and garnish with lemon wedges and parsley.

Serve with brown bread and butter. Tabasco sauce or cayenne pepper make a piquant addition.

CLARET

Although the wines classified as clarets are unquestionably French, the collective name given to them is just as unquestionably English. Here is Mrs Beeton on the subject:

All those wines called in England clarets are the produce of the country round Bordeaux, or the Bordelais; but it is remarkable that there is no pure wine in France known by the name of claret, which is a corruption of *clairet*, a term that is applied there to any red or rose-coloured wine. Round Bordeaux are produced a number of wines of the first quality, which pass under the name simply of *vins de Bordeaux*, or have the designation of the particular district where they are made; as Lafitte, Latour, &c. The clarets brought to the English market are frequently prepared for it by the wine-growers by mixing together several Bordeaux wines, or by adding to them a portion of some other wines; but in France the pure wines are carefully preserved distinct. The genuine wines of Bordeaux are of great variety, that part being one of the most distinguished in France; and the principal vineyards are those of Médoc, Palus, Graves, and Blanche, the product of each having characters considerably different.

WOODCOCK

Small it may be, and difficult to shoot because of the elusive way in which it flies to evade predators and shotgun pellets alike, but the woodcock is regarded by many as the finest-tasting game bird of all when it is well prepared.

It is not a common bird, but as Mrs Beeton informs us, 'The flesh of the woodcock is held in high estimation; hence the bird is eagerly sought after by the sportsman.' Her recipe for roasted woodcock offers a chance to savour the classic taste that made woodcock so popular with Victorian shooting parties.

INGREDIENTS—Woodcocks; butter, flour, toast.

Mode—Woodcocks should not be drawn, as the trails are, by epicures, considered a great delicacy. Pluck, and wipe them well outside; truss them with the legs close to the body, and the feet pressing upon the thighs; skin the neck and head, and bring the beak round under the wing. Place some slices of toast in the dripping-pan to catch the trails, allowing a piece of toast for each bird. Roast before a clear fire from 15 to 25 minutes; keep them well basted, and flour and froth them nicely. When done, dish the pieces of toast with the birds upon them, and pour round a very little gravy; send some more to table in a tureen. These are most delicious birds when well cooked, but they should not be kept too long: when the feathers drop, or easily come out, they are fit for table.

Time—When liked underdone, 15 to 20 minutes; if liked well done, allow an extra 5 minutes.

Average cost—Seldom bought.

Sufficient—2 for a dish.

Seasonable from November to February.

BAKEWELL TART

According to tradition, with which some food historians beg to differ, the White Horse Inn in the Derbyshire town of Bakewell, now the Rutland Arms, is the home of the original Bakewell Tart. This came about, the story goes, as a result of a mix-up by an inexperienced cook. Instructed by Mrs Graves, the landlady, to make a strawberry tart for visiting noblemen, the cook poured an egg mixture over the jam topping, instead of stirring it into the pastry mix, and then returned the tart to the oven. Mrs Graves' initial dismay turned to delight when her customers clamoured for more of the new kind of pudding. Another Bakewell lady, Mrs Wilson, wife of the candle-maker, managed to obtain the recipe and got busy making Bakewell Puddings – and 'The Old Original Pudding Shop' is still doing a brisk trade from her original site.

Ingredients

For the pastry:

200g plain flour • 100g butter • 2 egg yolks • 2tbsp icing sugar

For the filling:

100g softened butter

125g caster sugar

150g ground almonds

3 eggs

2½tsp almond essence

6tbsp strawberry or raspberry jam

25g flaked almonds

Directions

Place the pastry ingredients (except the egg yolks) in a food processor and pulse until the mixture resembles fine bread crumbs. Add half the beaten egg yolk and mix, then gradually add the remainder until the pastry forms a soft but not sticky ball. Cover in clingfilm and place in the refrigerator for half an hour or so.

Remove from the fridge and roll out on a floured surface, then use to line a 20cm loose-bottomed, greased, flan tin. Prick all over with a fork, line with baking parchment and cover with baking beans (if you have them, or uncooked rice, if not). Bake for fifteen minutes at gas mark 5 or 190°C, then remove the baking parchment and beans (or rice) and bake for another five minutes until pale golden in colour.

For the filling, beat the sugar and butter until pale and fluffy, gradually adding the beaten eggs and mixing well. Tip in the almond essence and fold in the ground almonds and again, mix well.

Cover the bottom of the pastry case with the jam and spoon the filling on top, evening out the surface until level, and sprinkle with the flaked almonds. Place the tart on a baking sheet and put in the middle of the oven for about half an hour until the filling is golden and firm to the touch.

When cool, remove from the tin and dust with icing sugar.

PORRIDGE

Food doesn't come much more basic or more nutritious than porridge. Grains, most commonly oats, could be cracked or crushed open without having to be finely milled. With the addition of water and the application of heat, an easily digestible, slow-release source of energy was created with the minimum of fuss or expense. To this hot gruel could be added all sorts of things to make it more interesting or heartening, but traditional porridge, as made for generations in Scotland, simply comprised oatmeal, water and a little salt – 'Chief of Scotia's Food', as Robert Burns described it.

Food on the move

If you wanted to indulge yourself and the family a bit, a bowl of cream was placed on the table and everyone dipped a spoonful of porridge into the cream before eating it. It became traditional, in fact, to eat porridge standing up, no one quite knows why, other than the entirely rational explanation that the sort of people who ate it were too busy to sit down. This staple fare could actually be made completely portable by being poured into a 'porridge drawer' and allowed to cool and set. It was then cut up into slices and taken out as a handy source of source of sustenance during the working day. On a practical level, slices of cooled porridge were easier to carry about than brittle oat cakes.

Once sugar became widely available the decadent habit of adding some to porridge firmly took hold. Less common (or less acknowledged) was the habit of adding a wee dram to one's morning bowlful. Another popular way to have porridge was to cook it in the traditional manner with water and a pinch of salt, and once it was in the bowl to pour round a 'moat' of milk.

Secret of the spurtle

Because of its excellent reputation as a highly nutritious food, porridge is once again popular with the modern health-conscious generation. In the early 1990s an annual World Porridge Making Championship started at Carrbridge, Inverness-shire and the top prize of the Golden Spurtle is hotly contested. For those who are unfamiliar with the term, a 'spurtle' is a wooden porridge stirrer. A spurtle is better than a spoon for keeping the porridge smooth, because the secret of making porridge is to keep stirring the mix as it cooks; cease stirring and the porridge can soon clog together in disagreeable lumps.

ETON MESS

This delicious dessert is now as much a part of the English summer as the smell of newly mown grass or the timeless sound of leather on willow. Originally served at the Eton College tuck shop in the 1930s, Eton Mess began as a blend of either strawberries or bananas with cream or ice cream; meringue was added later, as a distinct improvement in most people's opinion. It is now part of Eton's annual prize-giving celebrations, when boys and their parents and guests picnic together.

Ingredients

6 meringues
450g strawberries
375ml double or whipping cream

Directions

Chop and hull the strawberries, keeping aside a few as decoration. Whip the cream until it forms soft peaks, then fold in the strawberries and juice. Crush the meringues and fold these into the mixture. Spoon into wine glasses or sundae dishes and decorate with the saved strawberries. Serve immediately.

KIPPERS

Kippers are herring that are split open, gutted, salted and smoked, having been caught in the summer, just before spawning, when they are plentiful and still rich in nutritious oils.

There is evidence to show that herring formed part of the prehistoric diet from as early as 3000BC. No one knows how long people have been smoking food to preserve it, but it seems probable that they have been doing that too from remote times. In the nineteenth century many fishing ports on the North Sea coast and around the Irish Sea developed into flourishing centres for herring and kipper. Today, the Northumbrian fishing village of Craster, the Isle of Man and Loch Fyne, on the west coast of Argyll and Bute, are especially famed for the quality of their kippers.

Start the day with a kipper

Nutritionally, the herring and the kipper are bursting with goodness in the form of Omega 3 fatty acids, vitamins A and D, calcium and protein. They are also very low in toxins such as dioxins and mercury. Kippers are, therefore, an excellent choice at any time but particularly so at breakfast. Lightly grilled and served with brown bread and butter, or after a wholesome bowl of porridge, they provide an ideal start to the day.

ANGOSTURA BITTERS

Until 1846 the Venezuelan city Cuidad Bolivar was known as Angostura and it was there that a Prussian surgeon, Dr Johann Gottlieb Benjamin Siegert, developed a remedy for stomach troubles made from locally available herbs. Dr Siegert was the Surgeon General of the revolutionary army led by Simon Bolivar, *El Libertado*, in the early nineteenth century. The bitter medicine he prescribed was hard to take in its undiluted form and was always administered in a drink or in food.

It is, of course, the former idea that has proved so popular all over the world. To the British it is the essential ingredient to the one-time ubiquitous 'pink gin'. This was a drink especially favoured by the Royal Navy; sailors found it not only delicious but a cure for seasickness.

A closely guarded secret

All authentic bottles of Angostura Bitters will have been produced by The House of Angostura, which is now located on the island of Trinidad. The recipe is a closely guarded secret and known to only five people called 'The Manufacturers'; one of them is the descendant of the original Dr Siegert.

The label on a bottle of Angostura Bitters ensures the purchaser that the product 'imparts an exquisite flavour' to a wide range of dishes from fish to fruit salads, plum pudding to preserved fruits. However, a dash of Angostura Bitters is most commonly known as an ingredient in a number of celebrated cocktails, such as these.

Pink Gin

Pour a few dashes of Angostura Bitters into a martini glass or small wine glass and roll the liquid around, spreading it up the sides. Shake out any surplus bitters: only a trace is needed. Add a measure of chilled gin and stir.

Singapore Gin Sling

Created by the barman at the Raffles Hotel Long Bar in Singapore some time in 1915, this famous cocktail is made from:

$\frac{1}{2}$ measure gin
$\frac{1}{4}$ measure cherry brandy
1 drop Bénédictine
1 drop cointreau
$\frac{1}{4}$ measure orange, pineapple and lime juice
Angostura Bitters

Decorate with pineapple and cherry.

At Raffles this is topped with a little secret ingredient that ensures Singapore's celebrated hotel remains a place of pilgrimage for cocktail devotees.

SHEPHERD'S PIE

Shepherd's Pie was a Monday supper dish, using the last of the Sunday joint of lamb or mutton. Mutton is a rarity nowadays so the pie is nearly always made from minced lamb, either leftovers or bought as a pre-packed mince. A similar mashed potato topped pie using minced beef for the filling is called Cottage Pie – Shepherd's Pie obviously referring to its constituent meat. The thrifty nature of the ingredients means that the pie has been a mainstay for institutional chefs and a great filler for hungry school children. The best specimens have a tasty mince and a golden, slightly crusty topping.

Ingredients

For the filling:
450g minced lamb
1 onion, chopped
2 carrots, diced
1 stick celery, sliced
25g plain flour
300ml stock
1tbsp tomato purée
2tbsp Worcestershire Sauce
1 bay leaf
Salt and ground black pepper

For the topping:
700g potatoes
25g butter
50ml milk
Pinch of salt

Directions

Fry the lamb with the vegetables and bay leaf for about ten minutes. Sprinkle over the flour, stir well and cook gently for a minute. Stir in the stock, tomato purée and Worcestershire Sauce, season with salt and pepper to taste. Leave to simmer for about half an hour. Remove the bay leaf and tip the lamb mixture into an oven-proof dish. Leave to cool.

Meanwhile, boil the potatoes until tender and drain. Add the butter, milk and salt and mash until smooth. Carefully spread the potato over the lamb and roughen the surface of the topping with a fork. Cook in the oven preheated to 200°C or gas mark 6 for twenty to thirty minutes, until the filling is piping hot and the topping is golden.

PLOUGHMAN'S LUNCH

A mid-day meal of bread, cheese and pickle may have been the traditional meal for farm workers in the field for hundreds of years, but the name 'Ploughman's Lunch' was coined in the early 1960s when the English County Cheese Council hit on it as an advertising slogan.

Although there is little linguistic evidence to link this simple wholesome fare with ploughmen much before the late 1950s, the term perfectly captured the spirit of old England fostered by public houses in towns and cities as well as the countryside. Before long the Ploughman's Lunch, and later 'Ploughman's' on its own, was a permanent feature of the English public house menu.

Accompanied by a pint of beer or cider, the Ploughman's Lunch is a perfect showcase for landlords keen to promote local produce. Regional cheeses, locally baked bread to home-made pickles all find their way onto salad-garnished platters of Ploughman's Lunches across the country. Followed by a crisp English apple, and perhaps a second pint, the Ploughman's Lunch is a delicious, easily prepared treat that has become a firm favourite in pubs or on picnics everywhere.

SANDWICH

The idea of placing food between two slices of bread may not have been dreamed up by John Montagu, 4th Earl of Sandwich, (in fact the Romans were tucking in what amounted to sandwiches 2,000 years ago), but it was Lord Sandwich who popularized it in England and gave the 'sandwich' its name.

A universal debt

His lordship was an inveterate gambler, who would sit at the gaming-table for hours on end (once for twenty-four hours non-stop). Such was his passion for cards that he begrudged having to leave them for meals. So he got into the habit of calling for slices of meat between two pieces of bread, which he ate without the need to stop his card-play for more conventional meals. Convenience of this sort has delighted sandwich eaters ever since, as Woody Allen commented in *Getting Even*, when he said of the Earl of Sandwich, 'He freed mankind from the hot lunch. We owe him so much.'

Two hundred and fifty years later, of course, the sandwich has extended its culinary scope, with a medley of fillings and 'wrappings' which Lord Sandwich could never have envisaged.

PONTEFRACT CAKES

In 1760 an apothecary named George Dunhill experimented with a mixture of sugar and liquorice and produced a sweet that swiftly gained popularity locally and, before long, further afield.

Dunhill was based at the West Yorkshire town of Pontefract, which is now perhaps best known for the shiny black coins of liquorice, stamped with a picture of the town's castle. The fact that Master Dunhill lived in Pontefract is significant: it lay at the heart of the principal liquorice-growing area in the country. It is not surprising, either, that a man such as Dunhill, who practised as an early form of chemist, would produce such a sweet, because liquorice was primarily known for its considerable medicinal properties.

An ancient medicine

From ancient times, and in many parts of the world, the root of the liquorice plant was used to ease coughs and sore throats and to treat ulcers. Its anti-inflammatory properties also helped relieve pain and discomfort, especially that associated with arthritis. Liquorice roots were found in the famous tomb of the Egyptian pharaoh Tutankhamen, and the great Greek physician, Hippocrates, who lived four hundred years before Christ – known as the Father of Medicine – used liquorice for its healing properties.

From herb garden to factory

It is probable that the liquorice plant was introduced to the Pontefract area in the fourteenth century. It may have arrived with Dominican monks coming to Pontefract Priory, where it would have been planted along with other medicinal herbs. Some believe, however, that it was brought back from the Middle East by returning crusaders.

In due course the process pioneered by George Dunhill was industrialized to the point where there were thirteen factories at work in and around the town. The factory workers cleaned, ground and then boiled the liquorice roots, adding sugar and thickening agents. The raw mass was left to dry for about a week, then cut into blocks, pulled into strands and chopped into the coin shapes. Until the 1950s all Pontefract Cakes were hand-stamped by a team of forty-five workers, all women, who pressed up to 25,000 cakes a day. The last local harvests took place in the late 1960s or early 1970s and there are now just two producers of the famous sweet.

CORNISH PASTIES

According to West Country tradition the devil would never cross the River Tamar into Cornwall for fear he might end up as the filling in a Cornish Pasty.

Given the devil's connections with the underworld, his anxiety might have been well-placed because the pasty became a mainstay of the Cornish diet as the tin mining industry expanded and generations of Cornish miners worked underground every day sustained by one of the original take-away foods: their Cornish pasty.

A convenient hot meal all in one

Inside its pastry casing, a pasty is a convenient hot meal all in one, with meat, potato, onion and swede. Cornish tin mines were often equipped with large ovens at the surface, where the pasties could be kept hot until needed; to make sure that each miner collected the right pasty, his wife would mark the one she made for her husband with his name or initials before cooking it. The practical nature of the pasty even extended to its thick edges, which provided somewhere for a miner's fingers to grasp his lunch while he was eating it without the risk of his fingers, and the traces of arsenic sometimes found on them, touching his lips.

Observing traditions

Although other Cornish workers took to eating pasties, it was miners moving away from the county, as the tin industry declined, who helped spread the popularity of their native dish. (Interestingly no fisherman would ever take a pasty aboard his boat for fear of bad luck – perhaps the devil did cross the Tamar after all.) Other superstitions saw miners leaving the edges and corners of their pasties for the subterranean little people known as Knockers, who were thought to inhabit the mines and who were presumably 'bought off' with daily portions of pasty crust.

Cornwall must have seen millions of pasties made and eaten during the centuries, though few can have rivalled the thirty-two foot long giant pasty made by a group of young farmers in 1985. One possible contender to the record may have been another monster pasty made by bakers in Falmouth in 1999, when the town held its first pasty festival. On a day-to-day level, though, pasties can now be enjoyed with all kinds of delicious fillings, which makes it perfectly understandable that the pasty is now Cornwall's most successful export.

WELSH RAREBIT

When 'Welsh Rarebit' was first coined, it was called 'Welsh Rabbit', and so the dish of melted cheese and seasoning, poured over buttered toast was until the end of the eighteenth century when 'rabbit' was changed to 'rarebit'. The reason for this appears to have been lexical interference from a dictionary compiler who could find no connection between the dish and a rabbit, and decided to change the name to something more appropriate. The name 'Welsh Rarebit' has stuck, but had 'Welsh Rabbit' become as widely used it would have sat happily in the dictionary alongside other anomalies like 'Bombay Duck', which is really a fish, and 'Mock Turtle Soup' which is made from a calf's head.

Variants of this popular savoury dish are found else-where in the British Isles, but it is the Welsh version that has claimed ascendancy – and true Welsh Rarebit should never be confused with mere cheese on toast. Cheese (preferably Caerphilly cheese) and toast (ideally good quality whole-grain bread) are unquestionably the main ingredients, but what sets Welsh Rarebit apart is the addition of beer or milk, mustard, pepper and Worcestershire Sauce.

BARLEY WATER

Barley Water is an old-fashioned drink that is still considered valuable for certain medical conditions. It is also a popular summer drink associated with tennis parties, afternoons spent gardening and family picnics.

Ingredients

25g pearl barley
1 litre water
Pared rind of 1 lemon
Juice of 2 lemons
Sugar

Directions

Place the pearl barley in a saucepan with enough cold water to cover and bring to the boil. Drain, then replace the barley in the pan and add 1 litre water with the pared lemon rind. Bring to the boil, reduce the heat and cover the pan. Simmer for twenty minutes, then leave to cool. Strain the liquid and add the lemon juice with sugar to taste. Serve chilled.

LONDON DRY GIN

London and gin have a long association (and not always for the best or most reputable reasons) but since the second half of the nineteenth century London Dry Gin has established a universally acknowledged pre-eminence as the gin of choice for cocktail drinkers and those who enjoy the ubiquitous gin and tonic.

So why 'dry gin'? As with other drinks, the name distinguishes it from sweetened varieties. In the case of gin, the sweetener was added sugar – for gin, unlike most other spirits, derives its flavour from added ingredients. Brandy gets its flavour from grapes, whisky from malt, rum from molasses. London Dry Gin starts as a pure spirit, however, with the basic alcohol distilled from any sugar source: in practice this tends to be crops such as maize and barley. This is redistilled twice and flavouring ingredients are added before the mix is diluted with water to achieve the correct alcohol content for its respective markets: 40% ABV proof for home sales, 48% ABV for export.

Closely guarded formulae

Principal among the flavouring ingredients is juniper, followed by coriander and much smaller quantities of botanical ingredients like angelica root, calamus, coriander seeds and orris powder, which range in variety and percentage according to the closely guarded formulae of brand owners.

The term 'gin' was probably arrived at, like many brought to the UK from other countries, as a result of linguistic confusion. When English soldiers serving in the Low Countries in the sixteenth century began to acquire a taste for the local 'aquavit' spirit (as a result of which we have the term 'Dutch courage') they enquired after its name and were told it was *jenever* (sometimes spelt *genever*), from the French for 'juniper', *genièvre*. It didn't take long for the word to become Anglicized as gin, and it didn't take long for gin to become hugely popular. In 1690 half a million barrels of gin were consumed. By 1729 that had risen nearly tenfold.

In the Cities of London and Westminster one in four houses were thought to be selling gin, most of it probably deplorable. A series of laws were passed in the following century and a half to curb the appalling excesses reaped by wide-scale gin consumption and by the 1880s gin was well on the way to gaining the respectability and sophistication it enjoys today – with the best of London Dry Gin being distilled in London itself.

SHORTBREAD

Traditionally eaten to welcome in the New Year, shortbread is a popular biscuit in Scotland (and throughout the rest of the UK) as an accompaniment to a warming drink at other times of the year as well.

Ingredients

250g plain flour
175g butter
75g icing sugar

Directions

Cream the butter and icing sugar, then mix in the plain flour. Press into two 15cm, greased round sandwich tins and prick all over. Chill for thirty minutes. Mark the edge with a fork and cut into six wedges. Bake at 160ºC for fifty to sixty minutes. Cool in the tin for fifteen minutes, then on a wire rack.

SKATE

Skate, like several other fish, is less widely eaten than it was in the nineteenth century, when Mrs Beeton described it as being 'cheap and abundant in the fishing towns of England'. Her recipe for Skate with Caper Sauce captures the taste and tradition of those bygone days:

INGREDIENTS — 2 or 3 slices of skate, ½ pint of vinegar, 2 oz. of salt, ½ teaspoonful of pepper, 1 sliced onion, a small bunch of parsley, 2 bay-leaves, 2 or 3 sprigs of thyme, sufficient water to cover the fish.

Mode—Put in a fish-kettle all the above ingredients, and simmer the skate in them till tender. When it is done, skin it neatly, and pour over it some of the liquor in which it has been boiling. Drain it, put it on a hot dish, pour over it caper sauce, and send some of the latter to table in a tureen.

Time—½ hour.

Seasonable from August to April.

Note—Skate may also be served with onion sauce, or parsley butter.

BLACK PUDDING

What started out as a North Country speciality has gained popularity throughout the country, particularly as part of the Full English Breakfast. Other countries have their own versions: in Ireland drisheen, in France *boudin noir*, in Germany *blutwurst* and in Spain *morcilla*.

Black Pudding is basically a large sausage made black by the high content of pig's blood, which, with pork fat and oatmeal, is held together in a length of intestine. Aficionados will look for a sausage with plenty of specks of white fat in it.

The pudding's origins are lost in the mists of time – it's one of those products that grew out of the need to make use of everything that the slaughtered animal had to offer, including its blood. The great poet Homer, writing in the eighth or seventh century BC, makes a reference to something similar in the *Odyssey*: 'As when a man beside a great fire has filled a sausage with fat and blood and turns it this way and that.'

The following suggestion is a deliciously hearty way to start the day, especially if it's for a late weekend breakfast.

Ingredients

Black pudding, thickly sliced
Some large flat mushrooms
Eggs
Thick rashers of bacon
Slices of toast or fried bread or half a muffin

Directions

Grill or fry the Black Pudding, mushrooms and rashers, cover and keep warm. Poach the eggs until just set. Make a tower of the ingredients, starting with the bread or muffin, then (per serving) a slice of black pudding, a mushroom, a rasher folded and the egg on the top.

DEVILS ON HORSEBACK

Devils on Horseback may have started out as the same thing as their heavenly counterpart, Angels (made with oysters), but with the addition of some hellishly hot Tabasco sauce, which made them 'devilled'.

These days, however, they are less expensive hors d'eouvres comprising prunes or sometimes dates, stuffed with tasty morsels such as cheese, olives or almonds. The most usual stuffing is mango chutney. The prune or date makes the whole thing appear darker and, again, more devilish. Like Angels they are wrapped in bacon.

Ingredients

2 dozen soaked prunes, stones removed
12 rashers rindless streaky bacon
Mango chutney

Directions

Slit open a prune and insert some chutney and wrap in half a rasher of bacon. As each is prepared, pack them tightly in a baking tray and bake for about eight to ten minutes at 200°C or gas mark 6.

BREAD AND BUTTER PUDDING

A firm, golden crust with jagged edges on top and a sweet, soft, custardy under side are the hallmarks of the perfect Bread and Butter Pudding. Modern chefs have developed the basic recipe into a posher dessert fit for expensive restaurants with the addition of fresh fruit, chocolate, orange, or liqueurs. What follows is a recipe for bread and butter pudding 'as mother made it'.

Ingredients

6–8 slices of good quality white bread • 50g softened butter
50g raisins • 100g sultanas • 3 eggs • 50g caster sugar
550ml milk • zest of 1 lemon • 25g demerara sugar

Directions

Heat the oven to 180°C or gas mark 4. Butter the bread and cut into triangles. Butter a shallow dish, fill with layers of bread triangles, scattering the dried fruit between the layers. Whisk together the milk, eggs, lemon zest and caster sugar and pour over the bread. Allow to soak for thirty minutes. Sprinkle demerara sugar over the top of the pudding and dot with a little more butter. Bake for thirty to forty minutes until golden brown on top.

MARS BAR

What do Mars Bars, pinball machines and the yo-yo have in common – apart from being fun? The answer is that they all arrived in the UK from the USA in the same year: 1932.

The Mars Bar, produced at the Mars company factory in Slough, was a sweeter version of the Milky Way chocolate bar that the company was producing in the US market. Chunky in composition, with bold packaging and sold for many years under the marketing slogan 'A Mars a day helps you work, rest and play', the Mars Bar established a masculine and sporty image which made it popular with men and boys alike. (It was only in the early twenty-first century that marketing changes were introduced to make the Mars Bar more appealing to female confectionery consumers.)

Epoch-making snack food

The businessman who started Mars, which is now an $18 billion business, was Frank Mars who, with his wife Ethel, began making and selling butter-cream sweets from their home in Tacoma, Washington State, in the north-west of the USA. That was in 1911. Nine years later, Mars and his son Forrest hit on the idea of producing a version of chocolate malted milk that could be enjoyed anywhere. The product they came up with was the Milky Way, to give their epoch-making snack food its North American name. When Forrest Mars brought it to Europe a decade later, it was given the name Mars Bar and has been called that ever since.

Into battle

During the Falklands War of 1982 concern spread among British fighting troops liberating the islands when it became known that the task force's entire supply of Mars Bars had been loaded onto one ship, which was then sunk.

From mid-April 2006 until the end of the Football Word Cup in July, Mars Bars sold in England were packaged in wrappers bearing the word 'Believe' to indicate support for the England team. With the interest shown by some US businessmen in leading English football clubs, the special Anglo-American relationship found new expression in this enduringly popular chocolate bar in the summer of 2006.

COLMAN'S
ENGLISH MUSTARD

Colman's have been making mustard in or near Norwich since the first quarter of the nineteenth century and the manufacturing principles have remained largely unchanged in that time. Today Colman's mustard is still a blend of brown and white mustard seeds, which are washed, crushed, sieved and gradually reduced to a fine powder that produces what must surely rank among the hottest mustards in the world.

The story of this very English culinary icon began in 1814, a little over twelve months before the Battle of Waterloo, when this advertisement was published in the *Norfolk Chronicle* on 7 May: 'Jeremiah Colman, having taken The Stock and Trade lately carried on by Mr Edward Ames, respectfully informs his Customers and The Public in general that he will continue the Manufacturing of mustards' – and continue he did.

Tradition and quality

By the middle of the century the company was employing over 200 people and the famous bull's head had been adopted as the firm's logo as a mark of enduring tradition and quality. In 1866 the distinctive red and yellow livery was introduced to the labelling and in the same year Colman's won the ultimate seal of approval when they received a royal warrant as manufacturers to Queen Victoria.

Further growth in the early years of the twentieth century saw Colman's acquiring the rival mustard manufacturer Keen & Son, which had been in business since 1742 and had established itself so comprehensively in the UK market that its name even entered the language in the expression 'Keen as mustard'.

Colman's, however were equally aware of the importance of branding in maintaining market share. For almost sixty years, between 1880 and 1939, the company issued special pictorial tins every year, with special additional tins to commemorate major national events, such as the coronation of King Edward VII and Queen Alexandra.

Mustard and much more

As a powder, Colman's mustard is a versatile condiment adding a special piquancy to sauces and soups, in addition to its more familiar contribution to enhancing the flavour of roast beef and cold ham. It's also available as a ready-made mustard with water, sugar, salt, wheat flour, turmeric and citric acid added to the mix.

SPOTTED DICK

Spotted Dick is an ever-favourite pudding, probably as old as Christmas Pudding and just as warming and comforting when served with custard on a cold winter day.

References to a pudding resembling Spotted Dick date back at least 200 years, although the origin of its unusual name remains open to conjecture. Some maintain that Spotted Dick derived from Spotted Pudding, by way of variants in which Pudding became Puddink and Puddick. Another theory gives the name Spotted Dog, linking the pudding with the Dalmatian dog, which arrived in England in the eighteenth century. 'Through the years the Dalmatian has had many nicknames among the British people,' states one authority on the breed. 'A few of these are the English Coach Dog, the Plum Pudding Dog, the Fire House Dog, and even the Spotted Dick.' The spots on the pudding would certainly make a natural association with the markings on the dog.

In 2002 Spotted Dick stirred interest in the British media when it was reported that a hospital in Gloucestershire had decided to rename it Spotted Richard on its menus to avoid embarrassing would-be takers; the fact that patients ordered their pudding by simply ticking a box seems to have escaped the management's notice. The name Spotted Dick was reinstated amid much hullabaloo some time later.

Ingredients

225g flour
1tsp salt
100g butter
50g sugar
100g raisins or dried currants
6tbsp water

Directions

Mix together flour and salt, then blend in the butter. Add sugar and raisins and mix. Now add the sugar. Roll it up like a Swiss roll. Grease some kitchen foil and seal it around the roll.

Place in a steamer and steam for one and a half hours. Serve with powdered sugar and custard.

THE FULL ENGLISH BREAKFAST

Weekend mornings or a few days at a nice little hotel are treats made all the sweeter by indulging in 'The Full English'. It's probably a good idea to schedule in a long walk at some point in the day after one of these, but that is, of course, purely a matter of choice. When the English breakfast was at its height, it was intended to fuel sportsmen about to take the field in pursuit of fox or pheasant and was provided by numerous household servants. By the end of the Second World War, domestic staff were in short supply and austerity was the order of the day. Even so, many a working man would have bacon and eggs, followed by toast and marmalade and a pot of strong tea to start the day.

Regional variations

There are numerous variations on the theme, some regional, as in Scotland where slices of haggis and oatcakes may well be included, and Ireland, where you may be served farls (a kind of scone), soda bread or white pudding. Strictly speaking, these would, of course, be the Full Scottish or Full Irish breakfasts, respectively. Some variations are simply a matter of individual taste. For example, for some the breakfast would be incomplete without baked beans, for others beans are not to be tolerated. Some people may have big enough appetites to include a first course of porridge or other cereal but what most people mean when referring to the Full English is – 'the fry up'.

Principal ingredients

The three principal ingredients are bacon, fried eggs and good butcher's sausages; these are sometimes augmented by black pudding slices. Other ingredients considered essential by many enthusiasts are a tomato halved, fried mushrooms (preferably recently gathered field mushrooms), baked beans and that most wickedly delicious item, fried bread. Condiments to go with the Full English Breakfast are usually English mustard, tomato ketchup or HP Sauce. In spite of the presence of fried bread, the Full English is not considered really full without a rack of freshly made toast, some butter and marmalade. Coffee is drunk with the Full English Breakfast but tea, in large quantities, is more traditional.

The meal is usually consumed in companionable silence, each concentrating on the feast before them with occasional glances at the newspaper or requests for the marmalade. As Oscar Wilde so memorably said: 'Only dull people are brilliant at breakfast.'

BOVRIL

In the 1880s a Scotsman called John Lawson Johnston invented a brew, which he initially called 'Johnston's Fluid Beef', as a response to Napoleon III's plea for beef to feed his army. The logistics of provisioning them with meat in its usual form was proving to be too much of a problem, so Johnston hit on the idea of rendering it down into a concentrated form that could be made into a comforting and nourishing drink with the addition of hot water.

Strange to think of the British introducing the French to something in the culinary line, especially considering the homely nature of Britain's 'beef tea'. Stranger, yet, is the name Bovril. John Johnston took the Latin word for 'beef', *bos*, (which was standard practice when devising a trade name) and he then used a word found in a popular fantasy novel of the time, Bulwer-Lytton's *The Coming Race*: 'Vril' being an elixir used by a fictional race of beings to give them superhuman powers.

Bovril proved to be a huge success. It played an important part in feeding the nation during two World Wars and became a particular favourite, in more innocent times, with football fans. Rangers Football Club have a stand called the Bovril Stand because of the large advertisement for Bovril that it displayed.

Bovril can be used like Marmite: spread on toast, or added to soups and casseroles. Those who like it in its drink form, also like to try it with seasonings of pepper or cayenne to make it an even more warming beverage.

BLACK VELVET

Otto von Bismarck, first Chancellor of Germany, was famous for many reasons, not least for having a battleship named after him in 1939. A more obscure fact about this nineteenth-century statesman is his penchant for Black Velvet. Indeed, in Germany the drink is commonly called a Bismarck.

However, the drink was concocted in honour of another nineteenth-century figurehead of German extraction, Queen Victoria's consort, Prince Albert. Brook's, the London gentlemen's club, invented Black Velvet as their tribute to Albert in 1861, the year of his death.

Making real Black Velvet is a skilful job. Cold stout, usually Guinness, is poured very carefully into a tilted flute glass up to a little below the halfway point. If there is a head on the stout it should be left to settle. Then cold champagne is equally carefully poured to fill the glass. The aim is to float the champagne on top of the beer, keeping the two liquids layered, rather than mixed, in the glass. Pouring the champagne over the back of a spoon will help to achieve the desired effect.

For the sake of economy, other sparkling wines may be used and there is also Poor Man's Black Velvet – a mix of stout and cider.

HOT CROSS BUNS

The tradition of eating small cakes marked with a cross in the spring dates back to pre-Christian times. Pagan Greeks and Romans tucked into cakes of this kind as part of their celebrations of the Vernal equinox. The early Saxons followed a similar tradition of eating small wheaten cakes at around the same date in March.

In England there is a tradition that something resembling the present-day Hot Cross Bun was given to the poor at St Alban's Abbey on Good Friday 1361; from there, it is said, the tradition of eating Good Friday cakes spread to other places. What is certain is that Hot Cross Buns were well established in England by the early eighteenth century and have remained so ever since.

One a penny two a penny

In days gone by Hot Cross Buns were made early on Good Friday morning by housewives who rose before dawn in order to have them ready in time for breakfast. Bakers preparing commercial-sized batches used to work through the night to have buns ready for sale early on Good Friday. In London and other cities street vendors could be heard from an early hour, offering freshly-baked buns for sale from trays and baskets covered by blankets and white cloths to preserve the heat, and their cry became incorporated into the well-known nursery rhyme:

> *Hot cross buns! Hot cross buns!*
> *One a penny two a penny – Hot cross buns*

If you have no daughters, give them to your sons
One a penny two a penny –Hot cross buns

One old belief maintains that a Hot Cross Bun made on Good Friday itself will never go mouldy. Its properties were said to go further. Ailments such as dysentery, whooping cough, diarrhoea and the indisposition known as 'summer sickness' could apparently be cured by true Good Friday Hot Cross Buns. It was common until well into the twentieth century for a few buns to be kept each year, hardened in the oven and hung from the kitchen ceiling until they were needed. When someone in the household was taken ill, a portion of preserved bun was finely grated and mixed with water or milk for the patient to drink.

CHRISTMAS PUDDING

Christmas has been a time of special feasting in England since the Middle Ages, although the traditional Christmas Pudding (or Plum Pudding) as we know it today came into being during the seventeenth century.

At first dried plums or prunes were the principal ingredients, which his how the puddings came to be named after them. Even when raisins, currants and sultanas replaced plums, the name stuck, as did many of the traditions that had evolved over centuries of Christmases.

Stir-up Sunday

The Sunday before Advent Sunday (which is also the last Sunday in the Church Year) has a collect, or main prayer, which begins with the words 'Stir-up, O Lord, the wills of thy faithful people'. This was the Sunday when Christmas puddings were made and for obvious reasons it acquired the nickname Stir-up Sunday.

According to one superstition the pudding had to be made with thirteen ingredients to represent Jesus and his disciples. Every member of the family had to help mix the pudding with a wooden spoon, stirring from east to west in honour of the wise men of the nativity story.

Superstition and tradition

Other Christian symbols find their way onto a Christmas Pudding when it rounds off a meal on Christmas Day. The decorative sprig of holly which tops off the pudding is said to be a reminder of the crown of thorns worn by Jesus when he went to his crucifixion on Good Friday. In the Middle Ages, holly was also thought to bring good luck and it was widely believed to have healing powers, which is why it was often planted near houses to protect the inhabitants. Putting a silver coin in the pudding is another age-old custom that is said to bring luck to the person who finds it.

These days Christmas Puddings take the shape of the basins in which they are cooked, but many traditional puddings are depicted as ball-shaped. The difference in appearance reflects variations in cooking. Before the use of pudding basins, puddings, including Christmas Puddings, were wrapped in cloth and suspended in boiling water in a large pot until they were cooked, in the course of which the ingredients expanded, giving the pudding its distinctive round shape.

PIGEON PIE

Today most people see pigeons as more nuisance than nourishment, but this wasn't always the case. Until 1730, when the agricultural innovator 'Turnip' Townsend introduced English farmers to the practice of growing root crops to feed livestock through the winter, most animals kept for meat were slaughtered in November and eaten at once or salted down for later consumption. In their absence, pigeons were a constant source of fresh meat and during the hard winter months virtually the only fresh meat available from domestic sources.

Dovecotes, in which pigeons were kept, were once restricted to the well-to-do. They were built in the grounds of manor houses, or in those belonging to churches or other ecclesiastical holdings. Large dovecotes with upwards of 450 pairs of pigeons were capable (in theory) of producing over three tons of meat every year because of the pigeon's exceptionally short breeding cycle.

Changes in agriculture and changes in eating habits have seen a marked decline in the consumption of pigeon meat. At one time there were 26,000 working dovecotes in England; today only a small fraction of those remain. That doesn't make a well-made Pigeon Pie any less delicious, however, as this recipe by Mrs Beeton confirms:

INGREDIENTS—1–½ lb. of rump-steak, 2 or 3 pigeons, 3 slices of ham, pepper and salt to taste, 2 oz. of butter, 4 eggs, puff crust.

Mode—Cut the steak into pieces about 3 inches square, and with it line the bottom of a pie-dish, seasoning it well with pepper and salt. Clean the pigeons, rub them with pepper and salt inside and out, and put into the body of each rather more than ½ oz of butter; lay them on the steak, and a piece of ham on each pigeon. Add the yolks of 4 eggs, and half fill the dish with stock; place a border of puff paste round the edge of the dish, put on the cover, and ornament it in any way that may be preferred. Clean three of the feet, and place them in a hole made in the crust at the top: this shows what kind of pie it is. Glaze the crust—that is to say, brush it over with the yolk of an egg—and bake it in a well-heated oven for about 1–¼ hour. When liked, a seasoning of pounded mace may be added.

Time—1–¼ hour, or rather less.

Sufficient for 5 or 6 persons.

Seasonable at any time.

OYSTERS

'You needn't tell me that a man who doesn't love oysters and asparagus and good wines has got a soul, or a stomach either. He's simply got the instinct for being unhappy highly developed.'

That was where the satirist H H Munro, better known as Saki, placed oysters in his pantheon of fine tastes – and he was not alone. By the time Munro was writing in late Edwardian England, oysters were going up in the world and becoming the preserve of the well-to-do as their numbers declined through over-fishing and pollution.

Oysters for breakfast

This wasn't always the case, however. For much of recorded history oysters were consumed as a form of simple, readily available sustenance; by the Victorian era pickled oysters were widely eaten by London's poor.

Since ancient times, though, oysters have been regarded as more than a source of nutrition. As far back as the second century AD Roman writers were extolling oysters as an aphrodisiac; a quality possibly borne out by the high levels of protein and zinc, which boost sex drive and stamina.

That reputation has remained undimmed. Casanova is said to have break-fasted on fifty oysters to sustain his priapic prowess, while Diane Brown, author of *The Seduction Cookbook*, maintains 'Oysters are so sensual just in their nature.

They have that slippery, slurpy sensation when you eat them that makes them very seductive.'

Precisely.

Skill with a knife

Enjoying oysters (for whatever reason) is all very well, but actually getting them out of the shell can be quite a challenge. You need a short-bladed, heavy knife to open an oyster shell. Protect your hand with a folded clean tea-towel. The cupped shell should be underneath to stop the juice from spilling. Insert the knife between the shell halves at the hinged end and twist it to prise them apart. Save the juice. A lot of people opt to have their oysters opened by their fishmonger, which is a great deal safer, if slightly less rewarding.

Oysters to be eaten raw must be absolutely fresh and kept chilled.

MALT WHISKY

According to the Scotch Whisky Association, their product is 'the drink of success, fashion and prestige, drunk and appreciated by people of taste and discrimination all over the world…

And yet it remains true to its origins in the remote glens of Scotland, true to its traditions of patient skill and craftsmanship handed down through the centuries, true to its name, *Uisage Beatha* … the water of life.'

Invaluable export and dollar producer

Sixty years ago the importance of whisky was well appreciated as Britain struggled to recover from the ravages of the Second World War. Prime Minister Winston Churchill, as enthusiastic a supporter of whisky as he was of champagne and cigars, sent a minute to the Ministry of Food in 1945 with the firm instruction, 'On no account reduce the barley for whisky. This takes years to mature and is an invaluable export and dollar producer. Having regard to all our other difficulties about exports, it would be most improvident not to preserve this characteristic British element of ascendancy.'

In its early history, whisky was not the fashionable drink it was destined to become. Three hundred years ago whisky was still regarded as fitting 'only for the most vulgar and fire-loving palates'.

Licensed to distill

Even by that time, however, there were already a few truly fine whiskies to be enjoyed by the discerning; one such was the 'real mountain dew of Glenlivet or Arran, to be offered to guests as sparingly as the finest Maraschino wine'.

Political and excise setbacks hampered the development of fine whiskies through the eighteenth century and it was only when licensed whisky distilling was permitted in 1823 that the Scotch Whisky industry as we know it today came into being.

In spite of the many excellent blended whiskies available, connoisseurs invariably head for a single malt, the product of a single, named, distillery. Here the flavours are highly distinctive, the nose highly individual. Within this group there will also be the many variations in taste, colour and style obtained by age and the type of barrel in which the malt whiskies are stored.

TURBOT

The turbot is a popular flatfish that was being sold in large quantities at London's Billingsgate market by the eighteenth century. For much of the nineteenth century, the price fetched for turbot could vary hugely due to the large difference week to week in the numbers being landed by fishermen.

This was how Mrs Beeton advised her readers to prepare and serve boiled turbot. As a coda, she supplied a word of caution on not being over hasty in discarding parts of the turbot that might normally be removed from other fish:

INGREDIENTS 6 oz. of salt to each gallon of water.

Mode—Choose a middling-sized turbot; for they are invariably the most valuable: if very large, the meat will be tough and thready. Three or four hours before dressing, soak the fish in salt and water to take off the slime; then thoroughly cleanse it, and with a knife make an incision down the middle of the back, to prevent the skin of the belly from cracking. Rub it over with lemon, and be particular not to cut off the fins. Lay the fish in a very clean turbot-kettle, with sufficient cold water to cover it, and salt in the above proportion. Let it gradually come to a boil, and skim very carefully; keep it gently simmering, and on no account let it boil fast, as the fish would have a very unsightly appearance. When the meat separates easily from the bone, it is done; then take it out, let it drain well, and dish it on a hot napkin. Rub a little lobster spawn through a sieve, sprinkle it over the fish, and garnish with tufts of parsley and cut lemon. Lobster or shrimp sauce, and plain melted butter, should be sent to table with it.

Time—After the water boils, about ½ hour for a large turbot; middling size, about 20 minutes.

Sufficient, 1 middling-sized turbot for 8 persons.

Note—An amusing anecdote is related, by Miss Edgeworth, of a bishop, who, descending to his kitchen to superintend the dressing of a turbot, and discovering that his cook had stupidly cut off the fins, immediately commenced sewing them on again with his own episcopal fingers. This dignitary knew the value of a turbot's gelatinous appendages.

CUMBERLAND SAUSAGE

Fat coiled ropes of sausage meat have had a close regional connection with Cumbria for the best part of 500 years.

Unlike most other sausages that are divided into links, the Cumberland Sausage is prepared as a continuous rope that has always been sold by weight or length. There are suggestions that it may have been brought to Cumbria by German miners who settled in the area during the reign of Elizabeth I. They were used to eating thick meaty sausages back home in Germany and continued the tradition when they put down roots in England. Another suggestion is that the coiled loop was the only practical way of combining all the ingredients in a single skin. Either way, the distinctive Cumberland Sausage was soon a favourite in the north-west of England.

Distinctive quality and flavour

In the past the sausage was more highly seasoned than it is today, probably because of the influx of exotic ingredients that flooded into Cumbria in the eighteenth century, when Whitehaven was the third largest port in the country. Black pepper, ginger, nutmeg, sugar, molasses and rum became major imports along with other foodstuffs and many of these new commodities were incorporated into local specialities, including the spicy Cumberland Sausage. Until half a century ago the Cumberland pig was the principal source of meat for Cumberland Sausages, which gave them a distinctive quality and flavour. Although the meat from other breeds of pig is used now, the Cumberland Sausage retains its individuality among British pork products.

Strong regional status

Throughout its history the authentic sausage has had a very high meat content – sometimes amounting to ninety-eight per cent coarsely chopped pork, although the usual blend will have at least eighty-five per cent content of both lean and fat meat. Recipes vary from butcher to butcher, with many still following ones which date back 200 years or longer. However, the growing popularity of Cumberland Sausage has led producers to seek European Union protection to ensure that traditional standards of quality and contents can be maintained. Along with other distinctive regional produce found throughout the EU – Parma ham, Melton Mowbray pork pies, Normandy cheeses, to mention a few – producers of Cumberland Sausages want their product to be recognized and protected under the PGI (Protection of Geographical Indication) directive.

PORT

Port is a sweet, fortified wine from the Douro Valley in the north of Portugal. The wine was given its name after the city of Oporto at the mouth of the Douro River, which was its main distribution point. Britain became one of the principal importers of port when the county was at war with France in the late seventeenth century. British merchants opened trading houses in Oporto, several of which still operate there to this day. In 1756 the Douro valley was established as an *appellation*, making it one of the oldest protected wine regions in the world.

Fortified for taste and travel

The steep sides of the valley have been terraced since Roman times in order to grow vines, but the ordinary wine produced from them tended to be rather harsh. The addition of brandy during the fermentation process 'stopped' the fermentation at a stage when the wine was still sweet and fruity, and also ensured that it travelled better.

There are several kinds of port, most of which is drunk as a dessert wine today: ruby, tawny, white and crusted are the more usual ones. Ruby is the most readily available. It is stored in casks for three years before being bottled and can be drunk quite promptly. Tawny port can be achieved by adding white port to ruby port, though connoisseurs would look for a tawny that has developed its warm brown hue from longer ageing in wood; a process that requires at least six years and one that also gives a delicious nutty quality to the wine. White port is usually drunk chilled as an aperitif, while crusted port is a blend of vintages, which is unfiltered, so it has sediment in the bottle and plenty of character.

The wine of philosophy

In times gone by, ladies would leave the dinner table before the port was served and leave the gentlemen to enjoy their cigars and 'the wine of philosophy'. One tradition still widely observed is the practice of 'passing the port', which ensues that it moves clockwise around the table from the host, after he has served the guest sitting on his right. This seems to have originated as a naval custom, but may have arisen from the fact that circling anything anti-clockwise was a way of invoking bad spirits.

Perhaps the last word should go to Samuel Johnson, the great eighteenth-century man of letters and dedicated port drinker, who held the view that 'Claret is the liquor for boys; port for men.'

PHEASANT

Probably the most widely enjoyed game bird in the UK, pheasant are in season from the beginning of October until the beginning of February. In her celebrated *Book of Household Management* Mrs Beeton gives this traditional recipe for roast pheasant, and quotes the French author and gastronome, Louis Eustache Ude on the nature of the popular game bird itself.

'It is not often that pheasants are met with possessing that exquisite taste which is acquired only by long keeping,' Ude wrote in *The French Cook*, 'as the damp of this [British] climate prevents their being kept as long as they are in other countries. The hens, in general, are the most delicate. The cocks show their age by their spurs. They are only fit to be eaten when the blood begins to run from the bill, which is commonly six days or a week after they have been killed. The flesh is white, tender, and has a good flavour, if you keep it long enough; if not, it is not much different from that of a common fowl or hen.'

INGREDIENTS—Pheasant, flour, butter.

Choosing and Trussing—Old pheasants may be known by the length and sharpness of their spurs; in young ones they are short and blunt. The cock bird is generally reckoned the best, except when the hen is with egg. They should hang some time before they are dressed, as, if they are cooked fresh, the flesh will be exceedingly dry and tasteless. After the bird is plucked and drawn, wipe the inside with a damp cloth, and truss it in the same manner as partridge. If the head is left on … bring it round under the wing, and fix it on to the point of the skewer.

Mode—Roast it before a brisk fire, keep it well basted, and flour and froth it nicely. Serve with brown gravy, a little of which should be poured round the bird, and a tureen of bread sauce. 2 or 3 of the pheasant's best tail-feathers are some-times stuck in the tail as an ornament; but the fashion is not much to be commended.

Time—½ to 1 hour, according to the size.

BENDICKS BITTERMINTS

'Intense' is the word most frequently used to describe these quintessentially English after-dinner mints. Unwrap the elegant dark green foil with the Bendicks name picked out in contrasting silver lettering. Between your fingers is a thick disc of crisp dark chocolate containing ninety-five per cent cocoa solids, so intensely bitter it is difficult to eat on its own. Bite into it, however, and you taste the firm fondant centre that itself is so intensely flavoured with a very strong peppermint oil that it too would be a challenge if eaten by itself. Brought together, though, the combination of tastes and textures is uniquely rewarding and unforgettable.

Birth of the Bittermint

The brand name 'Bendicks' was formed by combining the first syllables of the surnames of the company's founders: Mr Oscar Benson and Colonel 'Bertie' Dickson. They set up in business in 1930, taking over a small confectionery concern in Church Street, Kensington. The following year Lucia Benson, Mr Benson's sister-in-law, devised the daring recipe for a unique new mint chocolate which became the celebrated Bendicks Bittermint.

By the mid-1930s Bendicks had opened a new flagship shop in Mayfair and thereafter became Bendicks (Mayfair) Ltd. The location was quickly matched by a glittering clientele, led by the Duke of Kent, son of one king of England, brother to two others and the uncle of Queen Elizabeth II. In 1962, just over thirty years after the creation of the Bendicks Bittermint, the company's royal patronage was officially recognized with the award of a Royal Warrant, 'By appointment to Her Majesty the Queen.'

Classic elegance

Bendicks have broadened their range of chocolates over the years, all of them maintaining the same standards of quality and exquisite presentation that established the company's reputation in the first place. When it comes to classic elegance and the perfect conclusion to a perfect English meal, Bendicks Bittermints are in a class of their own – and long may they remain so.

MINCE PIES

Mince Pies have been part of the English Christmas celebrations since the Middle Ages. In medieval times, however, Mince Pies were large communal pies, rather than the small individual ones enjoyed today. The filling was different as well. Original mincemeat pies would have contained minced mutton rather than the spiced mixture of suet, plums, raisins, sultanas and currants familiar to us now.

When it came to cooking them, the pies were baked in long oblong dishes, in which the top often collapsed, making the pie look like a crib. This was perfectly in keeping with the nativity story and the resemblance of the pie to the stable manger in which the infant Jesus was placed. As a result of this association a superstition arose in the Middle Ages that it was bad luck to cut a mincemeat pie with a knife. For a similar reason, children were often the first to be given a portion, so that they could make a wish with their first bite.

Banned by Cromwell

For a brief spell in the middle of the seventeenth century, mincemeat pies were banned, along with other Christmas celebrations, by the Commonwealth government of Oliver Cromwell. They were reinstated after the Restoration. By the Victorian era the meat content had disappeared leaving the spicy fruit mixture. The pies had also reduced in size, to the small, round mince pies that have proved such a temptation ever since.

Royal favourite

The tradition of offering mince pies to carol singers and other visitors at Christmas time probably gave rise to their also being called 'wayfarers pies', although there has never been any suggestion that mince pies were charitable hand-outs to the needy. King Henry V was so fond of mincemeat pies that he was served one at his coronation in April 1413.

Although ready-made mince pies are often delicious and are sold in huge numbers every year, the tradition survives of making mincemeat at home using ingredients such as cooking apples, carrots, currants, raisins, sultanas, dates, candied peel, grated orange and lemon rind, spices, brandy and shredded suet. Mincemeat is usually made a month before it is to be used and if stored in airtight pots sealed with freezer tape will keep for a good year.

VENISON

Robin Hood and his companions in Sherwood Forest may be the best-known consumers of venison in British folklore, but venison has been enjoyed in Britain since prehistoric times.

At one time 'venison' (from the Latin verb *venari*, to hunt) was applied to the meat of any wild animal. Just to confuse things a little further, 'deer' was used in Shakespeare's day to describe small animals, such as rabbits and hares, that were hunted for their meat (a usage which probably stems from the German noun *tier*, animal). However, there is no mistaking the fact that today venison is the meat of deer, whether hunted or farmed.

A favourite of Mr Pepys

For centuries land-owners hunted in deer parks in which the game they pursued was strictly maintained for their sport and consumption; in many cases poachers went after venison on pain of death. Samuel Pepys was fond of venison as these entries in his diary record: 'At the Clerk's chamber I met with Simons and Luellin, and went with them to Mr Mount's chamber at the Cock Pit, where we had some rare pot venison, and ale to abundance till almost twelve at night, and after a song round we went home … Mr Moore and I and several others being invited to-day by Mr Goodman, a friend of his, we dined at the Bullhead upon the best venison pasty that ever I eat of in my life, and with one dish more, it was the best dinner I ever was at.'

A taste of Old England

Many cooks regard venison from roe deer (the smallest native species in the UK) as the best, although meat from fallow deer and red deer are both stocked by British game butchers. Venison is cooked in a similar manner to beef. Having less fat, however, it benefits from moist-cooking methods such as barding or marinating before cooking. A tip employed by experienced cooks is to serve venison on very hot plates as venison fat has a higher melting point than beef fat, while cold venison is far less appetizing than cold beef.

Juniper, gin, red wine, port, rosemary and redcurrant all provide flavours that are excellent partners in venison recipes. They may be a far cry from venison haunches roasted over open fires in times gone by, but they recall a taste of old England as few other dishes do.

CHEDDAR CHEESE

Cheddar Cheese comes from the county of Somerset, a name in itself redolent of warm, lush pastures. 'Somerset' means 'the people of the summer settlement' – where better to graze the cows that produce the creamy milk for one of England's great cheeses?

The whole area around the village of Cheddar is unique, boasting the country's biggest gorge, largest underground river, and a cave where Britain's oldest complete skeleton has been found. It is not known when cheese making began at Cheddar but it is a recorded fact that Henry II ordered over ten thousand pounds of Cheddar Cheese in 1170 at one farthing a pound. Not only did the land lend itself to dairy farming and cheese making but it also provided ideal storage for the product. The renowned caves at Cheddar remain a constant cool temperature, rather like a huge cellar, and in days gone by the cheeses were stored in them.

Mature for taste

Cheddar is a semi-hard cheese produced from pressing moisture from the curd. It is formed into a drum about fifteen inches in diameter and bound round the rim with cloth. Its natural colour is pale yellow and its texture should be slightly crumbly. As with many cheeses, the longer it matures, the tastier it becomes.

Unlike Stilton, Cheddar's name is not protected, which accounts for its many imitations. Local producers claim that the only real Cheddar is that made with milk from cows grazed on pastures in the village's vicinity, that it is made by hand

and that the cheese should be allowed to mature for at least a year in its cloth binding. The European Union, however, has established 'West Country Farmhouse Cheddar' as a protected designation origin, to qualify for which cheese must be made in the traditional 'cheddaring' manner (cutting the curd into slabs from which the whey drains) in the four designated counties of Devon, Dorset, Cornwall and Somerset.

The best cheese that England affords

In 1724, Daniel Defoe wrote a splendidly partisan piece about Cheddar Cheese in *A Tour of the Whole of Great Britain*: 'The goodness of the cheese is preferred, without all dispute, it is the best cheese that England affords, if not, that the whole world affords' – a sentiment shared by many, no doubt.

HP SAUCE

With its distinctive tangy taste HP Sauce has been enlivening British food for over a century. It dates from a time when food eaten by most British people was bland and monotonous. At the same time preparing home-made pickles and sauces was expensive and time consuming. So the addition of a dollop of spicy brown sauce straight from the bottle did wonders for almost anything served at British meal-times. This was particularly true during the First and Second World Wars, when rationing and food restrictions did little to improve the taste and variety of food on offer.

What's in a name?

The sauce was first distributed by a Nottingham grocer, F G Garton, who sold the recipe and the HP name in order to settle a debt with one of his suppliers. How the sauce acquired its iconic initials is a unclear. Some maintain they stand for the Houses of Parliament, which are depicted on the label, a soubriquet Garton gave to his sauce after discovering that it was being stocked in one of the restaurants in the House of Commons. Others hold the more prosaic view, that the initials stand for Harry Palmer, who may have originally invented the blend before selling it to Garton. Whatever the truth of the matter, HP Sauce quickly established itself at Westminster and further afield.

Harold Wilson, leader of the Labour party and prime minster in the 1960s and 1970s, was so partial to HP Sauce that it was nicknamed 'Wilson's gravy'.

Wilson didn't speak publicly about his likes and dislikes at mealtimes, but his wife Mary let slip to an interviewer that her husband was inclined to 'drown everything' in his favourite sauce.

Enduring popularity

Presumably in an attempt to boost sales in non-English-speaking countries, especially those where French cuisine held sway, for years bottles of HP Sauce carried a translation in French of the company's sales pitch.

In September 2005 fashion designer Paul Smith was commissioned to customize bottles of HP Sauce to go on sale in Harrods as part of the store's Truly British season; all 500 boxed sets sold out in three hours. When production moved to the Netherlands in the spring of 2007, the loss of this uniquely British icon made headline news.

THE BOAR'S HEAD

The wild boar has been a creature of legend for thousands of years and in many different parts of the world. Hercules hunted the Erymanthian Boar and the goddess Artemis sent a huge, ferocious boar to terrorize the people of Calydon. The Irish warrior, Fionn mac Cumhaill, contrived to have his enemy gored to death by a boar, and the Norse goddess Freya was in the habit of riding a boar evocatively named Battle Swine. The beasts' courage and ferocity made them daunting quarry in medieval hunts, with dogs, horses and huntsmen running the risk of serious injury or worse from a boar at bay charging at them and slashing with its sharp tusks. The wild boar was Richard III's heraldic device and was a popular symbol for bravery and strength.

Christmas centrepiece

Because hunting wild boar was such a dangerous sport, frequently requiring acts of bravery from the huntsmen, it is easy to see why the dead beast was the object of awe and reverence. Adult males can weigh two hundred kilograms (approximately four hundred pounds) and grow to nearly two metres (six feet) in length. In England the boar became the centrepiece of Christmas feasts held in manorial and college halls. The head in particular was treated with great ceremony. It was often announced with a fanfare and brought in on a platter, an apple or orange thrust between its jaws, garlanded and decorated with bay, rosemary and holly.

Boar's Head ceremony

The best-known Boar's Head ceremony still survives from medieval times at
Queen's College, Oxford. As it is brought into the college hall, a soloist sings the
verses of the Boar's Head Carol and the choir sings the chorus. The dish is then
placed upon the high table and the Provost carves slices for those seated near him.
It is then sent round the other tables to be carved for the less exalted members of
the feast.

The earliest published version of the Boar's Head Carol (the first verse of
which is given below) dates from 1521, but it had been around for many generations before that.

The Boar's Head Carol

The boar's head in hand bring I,
Bedecked with bays and rosemary.
I pray you, my masters, be merry
Quot estis in convivio

Caput apri defero
Reddens laudes Domino

CRUMPETS

Different regions of the country have different ways of referring to crumpets and it can get a bit confusing, especially as in some parts of the north of England they are called 'muffins'! In the Midlands they tend to be called 'pikelets', although a real pikelet is thinner and not as regular in shape. The crumpet referred to here is made with yeast and has a thick round shape. In the cooking, the surface on one side forms deep holes.

As early as the fourteenth century there is a reference to a 'crumpid cake' which meant a 'curled up' cake. The name may have come originally from the Welsh word for a pancake, 'crempog'. To call someone 'my little crumpet' was to use an old term of endearment until, that is, the 1930s, when it took on a rather grosser meaning.

Distinctive appearance

The distinctive look of a crumpet comes from the mixture being poured into rings on a griddle. As they cook, bubbles force their way to the surface leaving holes as they disperse. When the bottom is cooked they are flipped over and lightly cooked on the holed side. They are usually kept for a while before eating and toasted just beforehand. Whilst still hot from the grill or toaster, they are buttered, usually very generously. Many enjoy their crumpets like that but others like to add jam or honey.

A very bright clear fire

Crumpets are usually shop bought now but whether bought or homemade, few things compare on a cold winter's afternoon, perhaps after a bracing walk, to hot crumpets dripping with butter and washed down with fragrant tea. To that end, here are Mrs Beeton's tips for serving crumpets:

> To toast them, have ready a very bright clear fire; put the crumpet on a toasting-fork, and hold it before the fire, not too close, until it is nicely brown on one side, but do not allow it to blacken. Turn it, and brown the other side; then spread it with good butter, cut it in half, and, when all are done, pile them on a hot dish, and send them quickly to table. Muffins and crumpets should always be served on separate dishes, and both toasted and served as expeditiously as possible.

REAL ALE

'What two ideas are more inseparable than Beer and Britannia?' asked the eighteenth-century wit the Revd Sydney Smith, and who would question his judgement? There are few things more British than a pint of beer – unless it's a pint of real ale. In 1971, the Campaign for Real Ale (CAMRA) was started by four friends, who were alarmed by the trend towards ersatz, fizzy, mass-produced beer. Since then they and others have done an excellent job of reviving interest in more traditional kinds of beer.

Traditional ingredients

Real Ale, or cask-conditioned ale as it is also known, is kept in a container with the yeast still present. This ensures that the beer continues to ferment and is fresh, with a natural effervescence when drunk. The traditional ingredients are hops, malt, yeast and water with no artificial additives or processing. Real Ale consequently contains a surprising number of vitamins and, it is claimed by some, has similar health benefits to those obtained from red wine if consumed in moderation. The brewing process starts with malted barley. This is mixed with hot water, forming something that looks rather like porridge, and which is left to 'mash' for several hours. After that the liquid, or 'wort', is tapped off and boiled with hops in a copper. The wort is naturally filtered and cooled before the yeast is added. Brewers maintain their own yeast variety, which helps to lend their beer its individual char-acter. The beer is kept in conditioning tanks before being barrelled. It should be dispensed by a hand pump using gravity from the cask. Real Ale does require some skill and care on the part of the landlord in keeping it in good condition.

Saviour of independent breweries

The revival of interest in Real Ale has saved many independent breweries and spawned hundreds of 'micro breweries' in towns all over the country. In fact, Britain has more small breweries per head of the population than any other country, and they produce some thirty thousand barrels of Real Ale a year. Beer festivals are now annual events where all sorts of well known as well as more obscure ales can be sampled along with regional food, live music and other grass roots entertainments.

We will leave the last word to an American, as what Benjamin Franklin had to say on the topic cannot really be improved on: 'Beer is living proof that God loves us and wants us to be happy.'

Amen.

STEAK AND KIDNEY PIE

Steak and Kidney Pie is almost invariably the masculine choice when spotted on the pub's menu. There can be no contest when it comes to tender beef steak in a rich dark gravy, little cubes of kidney and flavoursome mushrooms, all concealed under a crisp, golden, buttery pastry lid. You know something is an icon when it has its own Cockney slang and Steak and Kidney Pie has no less than two examples – 'Kate and Sidney' or 'Snake and Pygmy'. These days, the pie is usually made with mushrooms but they are a modern substitute for oysters, which were originally used. The following recipe is a happy choice, having both items in the ingredients.

Ingredients

900g braising steak, diced • 225g lamb's kidneys, halved and cored

1 large onion, chopped • 25g plain flour

570ml beef stock • 100g flat mushrooms

6 oysters • 425ml stout (e.g. Guinness)

Bouquet garni • Salt and freshly ground black pepper

600g puff pastry • 1 medium egg, beaten

Directions

Fry the onion in 15ml of oil, lift out with a slotted spoon and put to one side. Heat a little more oil in the pan if necessary and fry batches of the steak and kidney until it is all well browned. Put all the meat and onions back into the pan and sprinkle the flour over. Mix well and leave to cook gently for a minute. Gradually stir in the stout and stock and bring to boiling point, add the bouquet garni and seasoning and reduce to a very gentle simmer. Allow to cook for a couple of hours, adding the mushrooms for the last quarter of an hour. If possible, leave the stewed meat overnight before continuing, otherwise allow to cool.

Remove the bouquet garni. Open the oysters and add to the meat with their juice, then spoon the meat and oysters into a one and a half litre pie dish with enough of the gravy to cover, keeping any excess. Roll out the pastry and cover the top of the pie dish, pressing the edges firmly onto the rim. Make a couple of incisions in the centre of the pastry and glaze the whole with beaten egg. Cook at 200°C, gas mark 6 for about half an hour. Lower the oven temperature to 160°C, gas mark 3. Cover the pastry with foil to prevent burning and cook for a further twenty minutes. Heat the excess gravy and serve with the pie.

TRIFLE

Hundreds of years ago, feasts in well-to-do households would have finished with a selection of light desserts or 'little trifles'. Possets, custards, flummeries and syllabubs decorated with shining fruits and flowers were served as a feast for the eyes as well as the palate. These were the antecedents of the English trifle that has delighted Christmas revellers, christening party guests and wedding anniversary celebrants for generations. Like anything well used, its reputation became a little tarnished over the years as cheaper and more speedily made versions parodied the finer examples. The best trifles, and there are many legitimate variations, are light affairs with real creamy custards, sponges flavoured with good sweet wines or liqueurs and fresh fruit.

Ingredients

For the custard:

280ml milk • 280ml single cream

50g caster sugar • A few drops of vanilla essence

5 medium eggs • 2 level teaspoons cornflour

For the base:

450g small strawberries • Sweet sherry

1tbsp icing sugar • 300g Madeira cake

175g good quality strawberry jam

For the topping:
425ml double cream • A few drops of vanilla essence

Directions

First make the custard: whisk together the eggs, sugar, vanilla essence and corn-flour in a basin. Pour the milk and cream into a saucepan, slowly bring to the boil then stir into the basin containing the egg and sugar mixture. Place the basin over simmering water in a saucepan and stir continuously until the custard thickens enough to coat the back of a spoon. Put the basin to one side, covered in cling film to prevent a skin forming.

Keeping a few strawberries for decoration, slice the rest and mix with some sherry and the icing sugar.

Take the Madeira cake and slice it into three along its length. Spread jam on the two bottom pieces and sandwich all three together. Cut into slices horizon-tally and use to cover the bottom and sides of a glass bowl. Sprinkle over some sherry, according to taste, and empty the contents of the bowl of strawberries into the middle of the sponge cake lining. Pour over the custard and leave for a mini-mum of two hours. Whisk the double cream with the vanilla essence and spread over the custard.

Decorate with the remaining strawberries.

CHELSEA BUNS

Plump with fruit, sinfully gooey and lightly dusted with icing sugar, Chelsea Buns have been a temptation and source of delicious gratification to cheerful guzzlers for three centuries or more. Eighteenth-century Chelsea was famed for its buns and three monarchs – George II, George III and George IV all bought them from the celebrated Chelsea Bun House, which used to stand in Jew's Road (Pimlico Road).

In its heyday, the Bun House was kept by Richard Hand whose buns moved one contemporary poet to describe them as:

Fragrant as honey and sweeter in taste!
As flaky and white as if baked in the light,
As the flesh of an infant soft, doughy and slight.

Good Friday Favourite

The success of Mr and Mrs Hands as bakers was exemplified every Easter when crowds of up to 50,000 people were said to gather outside their premises on Good Fridays. In the end the commotion caused by a throng of this size obliged Mrs Hands to take action and, at Easter 1793, she 'respectfully informed her friends and the public that in consequence of the great concourse of people which assembled before her house at a very early hour on the morning of Good Friday last by which her neighbours (with whom she has always lived in friendship and repute) have been much alarmed and annoyed … she is determined, though much to her loss, not to sell Cross Buns on that day to any person whatever but Chelsea Buns as usual.'

Even though trade fell off after the closure of the Ranelagh Gardens pleasure grounds in 1804, in 1839 (its last year of business) the Chelsea Bun House was still selling 240,000 buns on Good Friday.

Cambridge Blues

By this time Chelsea Buns were well established as national favourites, especially among ravenous schoolboys and students. The likes of Billy Bunter, the most famous schoolboy in English popular fiction, chomped their way through them at schools up and down the country. From the 1920s, those who went up to Cambridge would have found a ready supply of Chelsea Buns at the cake shop called Fitzbillies. Generations of undergraduates patronized this famous bakery whose celebrated produce still drew glowing testimonials half-a-century after their first appearace. 'Fitzbillies' Chelsea buns are light, succulent and sticky, rich with butter and currants …' reported one devotee. 'I have been unable to visit Cambridge without returning laden with buns to show Chelsea friends what the place has lost.'

PICCALILLI

The origins of both the familiar mustard-coloured pickle and its name are open to conjecture. Recipes date from the eighteenth century and, because of the presence of spices, they may have developed along with Britain's expansion into India and the East. The best explanation of the name is that it is a pun, perhaps on the words *pickle* and *chilli*. Piccalilli is a colourful, spicy accompaniment to cold meats, cheese and, especially in America, hot dogs and hamburgers.

As with many pickles and preserves, the best time to make piccalilli is in that season of plenty – the autumn. The following recipe comes from Yorkshire and dates from the early 1900s and makes a little under 1.5kg of piccalilli.

Ingredients

450g peeled button onions

675g cauliflower florets

550g chopped cucumber and/or courgettes

450g chopped green beans

3 red chillies cut into strips

225g granulated sugar

85g plain flour

2tsp allspice

2tsp turmeric

½tsp cayenne pepper

2tbsp mustard powder

2tbsp ground ginger

2tbsp mild curry powder

30ml black peppercorns

1.15 litres malt vinegar

Directions

Add 85g of salt to 1.15 litres of water and bring to the boil in a large pan. Put in all the vegetables and blanch for five minutes, then drain well, running them under cold water to cool. Put the sugar, flour and the spices (except the peppercorns) into a bowl with three or four tablespoons of vinegar and stir to form a paste. Put the rest of the vinegar, the peppercorns and the spice paste into a large pan and bring to the boil, stirring all the time. Lower the heat and cook for a little while until the sauce begins to thicken, still stirring. Take the pan off the hob and let it cool, stirring from time to time to get rid of any skin that may form. Combine the sauce and the vegetables in a clean bowl and leave in a cool place for twenty-four hours. After that make sure the vegetables are well mixed and covered with the sauce, then bottle and label. The end result is greatly improved if allowed to mature in a cool, dark place for a couple or more months.

COLLEGE PUDDINGS

College Puddings evolved in schools and university halls that catered for large numbers of students. Such establishments invariably had quantities of staling bread and utilizing this in a nourishing hot pudding satisfied a sense of thrift as well as providing sustenance for hungry students

This is Mrs Beeton's recipe for College Puddings.

INGREDIENTS—1 pint of bread crumbs, 6 oz. of finely-chopped suet, ¼ lb. of currants, a few thin slices of candied peel, 3 oz. of sugar, ¼ nutmeg, 3 eggs, 4 tablespoonfuls of brandy.

Mode.—Put the bread crumbs into a basin; add the suet, currants, candied peel, sugar, and nutmeg, grated, and stir these ingredients until they are thoroughly mixed. Beat up the eggs, moisten the pudding with these, and put in the brandy; beat well for a few minutes, then form the mixture into round balls or egg-shaped pieces; fry these in hot butter or lard, letting them stew in it until thoroughly done, and turn them two or three times, till of a fine light brown; drain them on a piece of blotting-paper before the fire; dish, and serve with wine sauce.

Time.—15 to 20 minutes.

Sufficient for 7 or 8 puddings. *Seasonable* at any time.

SCOTCH WOODCOCK

This savoury dish was popular in Victorian and Edwardian Scotland. It was served at the end of a meal then. Now you would be more likely to serve it as a starter or a light snack.

Ingredients

Serves: 4

4 large slices bread, toasted, crusts removed and buttered

15g butter

The Gentleman's Relish

150ml milk

4 eggs

Large pinch cayenne pepper

2 x 50g cans anchovies, drained

Directions

Cut the pieces of toast in half and spread with Gentleman's Relish.

Melt the butter in a pan. Whisk together the milk, eggs and cayenne pepper, then pour into the pan. Stir slowly over a gentle heat until the mixture starts to thicken. Remove from the heat and stir until it is creamy. Divide the mixture between the toasts. Top with the anchovy fillets, arranged in a criss-cross pattern.